W9-CIP-032

Florida edition

Ready® Classroom
Mathematics

Grade 5 • Volume 1

Curriculum Associates

NOT FOR RESALE

978-1-4957-6821-7
©2020–Curriculum Associates, LLC
North Billerica, MA 01862
No part of this book may be reproduced
by any means without written permission
from the publisher.
All Rights Reserved. Printed in USA.
1 2 3 4 5 6 7 8 9 10 11 12 13 14 15   20 19

Contents

Standards in boldface indicate the standards covered by the majority of lesson content.
See page A28 for full text of standards.

©Curriculum Associates, LLC   Copying is not permitted.

Contents (continued)

UNIT 2

Decimals and Fractions
Place Value, Addition, and Subtraction

©Curriculum Associates, LLC   Copying is not permitted.

UNIT 3

More Decimals and Fractions
Multiplication and Division

Standards in boldface indicate the standards covered by the majority of lesson content. See page A28 for full text of standards.

©Curriculum Associates, LLC   Copying is not permitted.

UNIT 4

Measurement, Data, and Geometry
Converting Units, Using Data, and Classifying Figures

©Curriculum Associates, LLC   Copying is not permitted.

UNIT 5

Algebraic Thinking and the Coordinate Plane
Expressions, Graphing Points, Patterns and Relationships

Standards in boldface indicate the standards covered by the majority of lesson content.
See page A28 for full text of standards.

©Curriculum Associates, LLC   Copying is not permitted.

Whole Number Operations

Volume, Multiplication, and Division

☑ SELF CHECK

Before starting this unit, check off the skills you know below. As you complete each lesson, see how many more skills you can check off!

I can . . .	Before	After
Find the volume of a solid figure by counting unit cubes.	☐	☐
Find volume by using a formula.	☐	☐
Break apart a solid figure into rectangular prisms to find its volume.	☐	☐
Multiply multi-digit whole numbers, for example: $410 \times 16 = 6,560$.	☐	☐
Divide a multi-digit whole number by a two-digit number, for example: $2,812 \div 38 = 74$.	☐	☐

Build Your Vocabulary

Math Vocabulary

Fill in the blank boxes using the review words.

$$\begin{array}{r} \boxed{} \\ \times\ \boxed{} \\ \hline \boxed{} \end{array}$$

$$\boxed{}\ \boxed{}$$

$$\boxed{} \times \boxed{} = \boxed{}$$

$$\boxed{} \div \boxed{} = \boxed{}$$

Using the review words, complete the sentence.

When you divide the .... 72 by the 8,

the .... is 9.

Academic Vocabulary

Place a check next to the academic words you know. Then use the words to complete the sentences.

☐ reasonable   ☐ result   ☐ justify   ☐ reason

1 You must .... your answer to prove it is correct.

2 The .... of multiplying two numbers is called the product.

3 She is a .... person; she is fair and sensible.

4 When you make sense of a problem, you .... and use what you know to help solve it.

©Curriculum Associates, LLC   Copying is not permitted

Understand Volume

Dear Family,

This week your child is exploring volume.

Volume is the amount of space inside a **solid figure**. A **unit cube** is a cube, 1 unit on each edge, used to measure volume.

Your child has already learned to find the area of a **plane figure**, such as a rectangle, by covering it with **unit squares**. Area is the number of square units needed to cover a plane figure.

Area = 4 square units

Now your child is learning to find the volume of a solid figure, such as a cube, by filling it with unit cubes. Volume is the number of unit cubes needed to fill a solid figure. The cube at the right has a volume of 8 **cubic units**.

Volume = 8 cubic units

Each unit cube in the solid figures *A* and *B* at the right has a volume of 1 cubic unit.

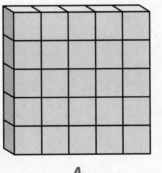
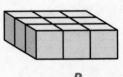

A   *B*

To find which figure has a greater volume, you can count the unit cubes. Figure *A* has a volume of 25 cubic units. Figure *B* has a volume of 9 cubic units. Figure *A* has a greater volume than Figure *B* because 25 > 9.

Invite your child to share what he or she knows about volume by doing the following activity together.

ACTIVITY VOLUME OF A RECTANGULAR PRISM

Do this activity with your child to explore volume.

A solid figure with six rectangular sides is called a **rectangular prism**. Work together with your child to find the volume of the rectangular prisms below.

- Each solid figure below is a rectangular prism made of unit cubes. Each unit cube has a volume of 1 cubic unit.

- Ask your child to explain how to find the volume of each rectangular prism. Then write the volume.

- Challenge! Look at all the solid figures below. Which two figures have the same volume? What is the same about the figures? What is different?

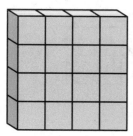

Volume = ... cubic units

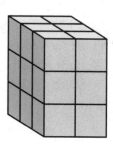

Volume = ... cubic units

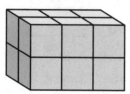

Volume = ... cubic units

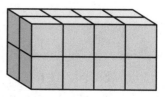

Volume = ... cubic units

©Curriculum Associates, LLC   Copying is not permitted

Explore Volume

What does volume measure?

Florida Standards

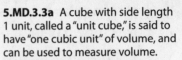

5.MD.3.3a A cube with side length 1 unit, called a "unit cube," is said to have "one cubic unit" of volume, and can be used to measure volume.

5.MD.3.3b A solid figure which can be packed without gaps or overlaps using *n* unit cubes is said to have a volume of *n* cubic units.

5.MD.3.4, 5.MD.3.5

MODEL IT

Complete the problems below to compare *area* and *volume*.

1 A **plane figure** is a two-dimensional figure. Explain how to measure the area of the plane figure using the **unit square**.

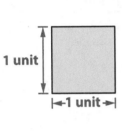

1 unit

|←1 unit→|

unit square

plane figure

2 A **solid figure** is a three-dimensional figure. The **volume** of a solid figure is the amount of space inside the figure.

A **unit cube** is a cube that has side lengths of 1 unit. How do you think you could use unit cubes to measure the volume of the solid figure?

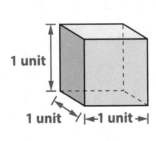

1 unit

1 unit |←1 unit→|

unit cube

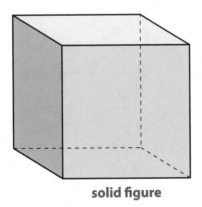

solid figure

DISCUSS IT

- Compare how you answered the questions about area and volume with your partner. How were your explanations alike and different?

- I think finding the volume of a solid figure is like finding the area of a plane figure because . . .

MODEL IT

Complete the problems below.

3 A **rectangular prism** is a solid figure with six rectangular sides, or **faces**. The two boxes shown below are identical rectangular prisms with unit cubes inside them.

Circle the diagram that you think shows the correct way to use unit cubes to measure the volume of the rectangular prism. Cross out the incorrect way. Then explain your choice.

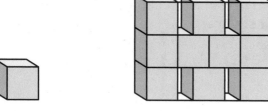

1 unit cube   **Way 1**   **Way 2**

4 A unit cube is said to have one **cubic unit** of volume. Cubic units are used to measure the volume of a solid figure.

a. What is the volume of each unit cube inside the rectangular prism you circled in problem 3? .... cubic unit(s)

b. What is the volume of the rectangular prism?

.... cubic unit(s)

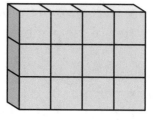

DISCUSS IT

• How did you and your partner each select the way to measure volume?

• I think when you measure volume with unit cubes, it is important to . . .

5 REFLECT

Why do you use cubic units instead of square units to find the volume of a solid figure?

....

....

....

....

©Curriculum Associates, LLC Copying is not permitted

Prepare for Volume

1   Think about what you know about units of measure. Fill in each box. Use words, numbers, and pictures. Show as many ideas as you can.

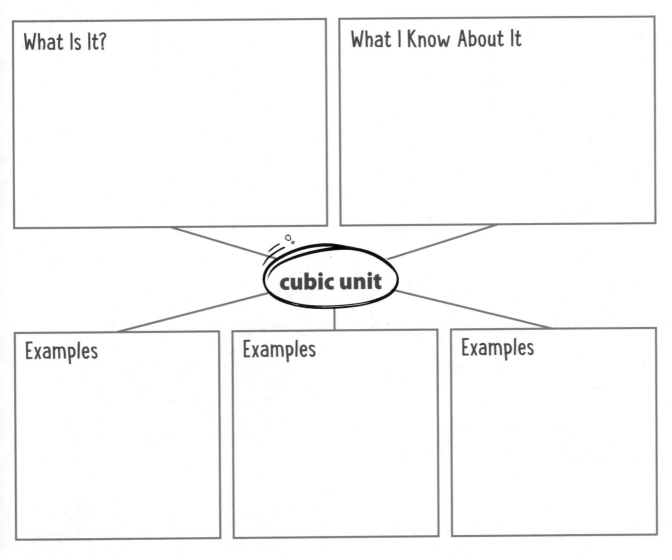

What Is It?	What I Know About It

cubic unit

Examples	Examples	Examples

2   Lamond says that the diagram at the right shows a solid figure with a volume of 6 cubic units. Is he correct? Explain.

Solve.

③ Mai uses unit cubes to help measure the volume
of a box. She thinks the volume of the box is
8 cubic units. Do you agree? Explain.

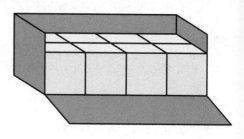

④ What is the volume of the rectangular prism?

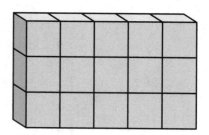

.... cubic unit(s)

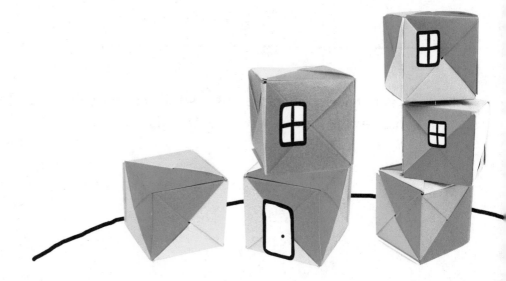

©Curriculum Associates, LLC   Copying is not permitted

Develop Understanding of Volume

MODEL IT: ADD TO FIND VOLUME
Try these two problems.

1 The rectangular prism shown below is made of unit cubes with no gaps or overlaps between the cubes.

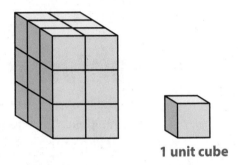

1 unit cube

a. Write an addition equation to find the volume of the prism.

b. Explain what each number in your addition equation represents.

2 Suppose you add another layer of cubes on top of the rectangular prism in problem 1. What would be your addition equation for the new rectangular prism? What would be the new volume?

DISCUSS IT

• How did you and your partner figure out how many cubes are in the whole prism if you cannot see them all?

• I think you can use addition to help you measure volume of a rectangular prism because . . .

©Curriculum Associates, LLC   Copying is not permitted

MODEL IT: MULTIPLY TO FIND VOLUME

Use multiplication to find volume.

3 The rectangular prism shown is made of unit cubes with no gaps or overlaps between the cubes.

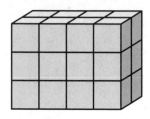

1 unit cube

a. Write a multiplication equation to find the volume of the rectangular prism.

b. Explain what each number in your multiplication equation represents.

DISCUSS IT

• Did you write the same multiplication equation as your partner?

• I think you can use multiplication to help you measure volume because . . .

CONNECT IT

Complete the problems below.

4 How are the addition and multiplication strategies for finding volume alike? How are they different?

5 Figure *A* and Figure *B* are built with unit cubes of the same size. Explain how to use the volume of Figure *A* to find the volume of Figure *B*.

A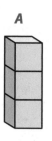

B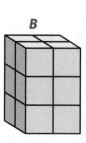

©Curriculum Associates, LLC   Copying is not permitted

Practice with Volume

Study how the Example shows counting unit cubes to find the volume of a rectangular prism. Then solve problems 1–8. Each figure shown is built with unit cubes.

EXAMPLE

Peter stacks unit cubes to build this rectangular prism. What is the volume of the figure?

There are 4 unit cubes in 1 layer.
There are 5 layers.

$$4 + 4 + 4 + 4 + 4 = 20$$
$$5 \times 4 = 20$$

There are 20 unit cubes.

Volume = 20 cubic units

1 layer

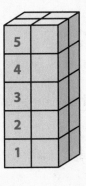

1. Look at Figure A and fill in the blanks below.

   There are _____ layers and _____ unit cubes in each layer.

   _____ × _____ cubes = _____ unit cubes.

   The volume of Figure A is _____ cubic units.

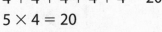

A

2. What is the volume of Figure B? Tell how you know.

B

3. Elena stacks 2 layers of 4 unit cubes to fill a small box.

   How many cubes are in the box? _____

   What is the volume of Elena's box? _____

©Curriculum Associates, LLC   Copying is not permitted

4 Look at Figure C and fill in the blanks below.

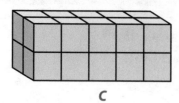

C

Vocabulary

unit cube a cube that has side lengths of 1 unit.

volume the amount of space inside a solid figure.

There are .... layers and .... unit cubes in each layer.

.... × .... cubes = ... unit cubes.

The volume of Figure C is .... cubic units.

5 What is the volume of Figure D?

....

D

6 Figures D and E are made from unit cubes of the same size. How many of Figure D does it take to fill Figure E? How does the volume of Figure E relate to the volume of Figure D? Explain.

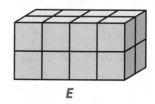

E

7 A prism has a volume of 36 cubic units. It has 9 layers of unit cubes. How many unit cubes are in each layer?

....

8 Draw or describe Box F that has a volume of 5 cubic units. Then draw or describe a box that has 3 times the volume of Box F. What is the volume of the second box?

Solution ....

©Curriculum Associates, LLC Copying is not permitted

Refine Ideas About Volume

APPLY IT

Complete these problems on your own.

1 INFER

Eli is stacking unit cubes in a box. He partially fills the box, pauses, and says, "The volume of this box is 18 cubic units."

Explain how Eli found the volume of the box.

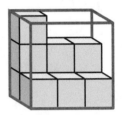

2 EXPLAIN

Zoe says that a box that is 1 unit wide, 2 units long, and 3 units tall has a greater volume than a box that is 2 units wide, 3 units long, and 1 unit tall. Is she correct? Explain your answer.

3 COMPARE

Each cube in Figures *A* and *B* has a volume of 1 cubic unit. Which figure has less volume, Figure *A* or Figure *B*? Explain your answer.

A

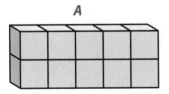

B

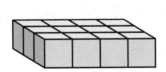

PAIR/SHARE

Discuss your solutions for these three problems with a partner.

Use what you have learned to complete problem 4.

4. Niles uses 16 blocks, each having a volume of 1 cubic unit, to build a rectangular prism.

Part A Draw or build a model to represent the situation.

Part B Look at your model. Describe the number of layers and the number of blocks in each layer. Then describe a different rectangular prism that also has a volume of 16 cubic units.

5. MATH JOURNAL

Heather builds a rectangular prism with 3 layers of unit cubes. Each layer of her prism has 10 unit cubes. Explain why the volume of Heather's prism is said to be 30 cubic units.

©Curriculum Associates, LLC Copying is not permitted

Find Volume Using Unit Cubes

Dear Family,

This week your child is learning to find volume using unit cubes.

Suppose you want to find the volume of the rectangular prism shown at the right. One way to find the volume is to fill it with unit cubes that each have a volume of 1 cubic centimeter.

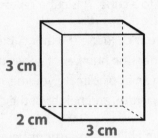

3 cm

2 cm   3 cm

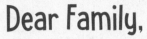

1 cm

1 cm   1 cm

1 cubic centimeter

You can count all the cubes to find the volume. The prism has a volume of 18 cubic centimeters.

3 cm

2 cm   3 cm

Another way to find the volume is to count the cubes in each layer and then add.

There are 6 cubes in each layer and 3 layers in all.

6 + 6 + 6 = 18 cubes

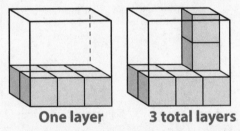

One layer   **3 total layers**

The volume of the rectangular prism is 18 cubic centimeters. Using either method, the volume is the same.

Your child is also learning that unit cubes can be different sizes. So, it is important to know the size of the cube you are using when you find the volume of a figure.

- A unit cube with side lengths of 1 centimeter has a volume of 1 cubic centimeter.

- A unit cube with side lengths of 1 inch has a volume of 1 cubic inch.

- A unit cube with side lengths of 1 foot has a volume of 1 cubic foot.

Invite your child to share what he or she knows about different ways to find volume by doing the following activity together.

ACTIVITY FIND VOLUME USING UNIT CUBES

Do this activity with your child to find volume with unit cubes.

Materials scissors, tape, household containers shaped like rectangular prisms, such as cereal boxes and tissue boxes

- Cut out the cube pattern below on the solid lines. Fold on the dotted lines and tape into a cube. This cube represents 1 cubic unit of volume.

- Have your child use the unit cube to estimate the volume of one household container (the number of cubes that fit in the container). Because your child is finding an approximate volume, discuss that the cubes do not need to fill the length, width, and height of the container completely (with no gaps).

- Ask your child the questions below:

  How many cubes would fit in the bottom of the box?
  How many layers of cubes would fit in the box?
  What is the approximate volume of the box?

- Repeat for another container.

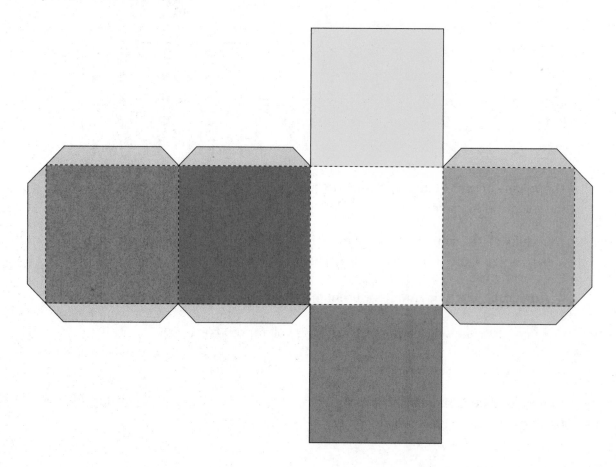

©Curriculum Associates, LLC   Copying is not permitted

Explore Finding Volume Using Unit Cubes

Previously, you learned that you can fill a solid figure with unit cubes to find its volume. Use what you know to try to solve the problem below.

> **Carl filled the clear box shown below with unit cubes to find its volume. The unit cubes Carl used all have side lengths of 1 foot. What is the volume of the box?**
>
>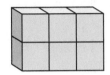
>
> 1 ft
> 1 ft 1 ft

Florida Standards

5.MD.3.4 Measure volumes by counting unit cubes, using cubic cm, cubic in, cubic ft, and improvised units.

5.MD.3.5a Find the volume of a right rectangular prism with whole-number side lengths by packing it with unit cubes, and show that the volume is the same as would be found by multiplying the edge lengths, equivalently by multiplying the height by the area of the base. Represent threefold whole-number products as volumes.

5.MD.3.3a, 5.MD.3.3b

TRY IT

 **Math Toolkit**
- unit cubes
- grid paper
- isometric dot paper
- square sticky notes

 **DISCUSS IT**

Ask your partner: How did you get started?

Tell your partner: I started by . . .

CONNECT IT

1 LOOK BACK

Describe the measurement unit Carl should use and explain how he can find the volume of the box.

2 LOOK AHEAD

Volume is measured in cubic units. Here are some cubic units you might use to measure volume.

Unit of Volume	cubic inch	cubic centimeter	cubic foot
Unit Cube	1 in. 1 in. 1 in.	1 cm 1 cm 1 cm	1 ft 1 ft 1 ft

Carl has another box as shown below. What is its volume? ....

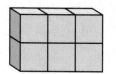

1 in. 1 in. 1 in.

3 REFLECT

What is the same and what is different about the volume of Carl's two boxes?

....

....

....

....

Prepare for Finding Volume Using Unit Cubes

1 Think about what you know about solid figures. Fill in each box.
Use words, numbers, and pictures. Show as many ideas as you can.

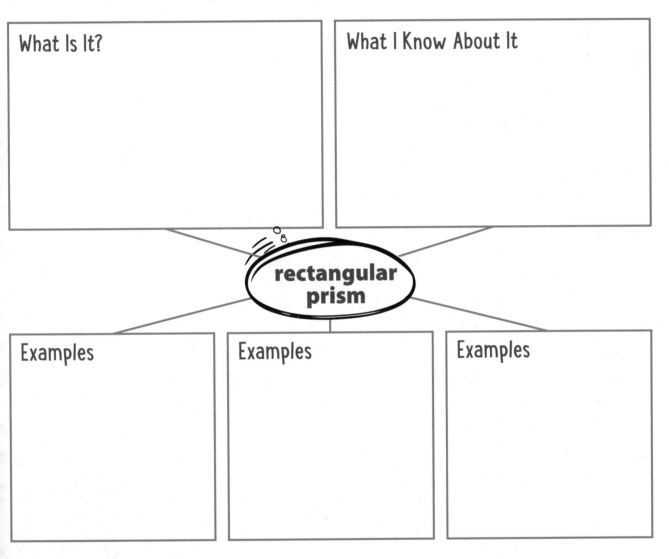

| What Is It? | What I Know About It |

rectangular prism

| Examples | Examples | Examples |

2 These two rectangular prisms are filled with unit cubes of the same size.

Do the prisms have the same volume? Explain.

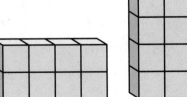

©Curriculum Associates, LLC   Copying is not permitted

3 Solve the problem. Show your work.

Jan filled the box shown below with unit cubes to find its volume. The unit cubes Jan used all have side lengths of 1 centimeter. What is the volume of the box?

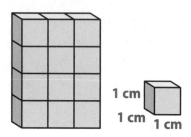

1 cm
1 cm 1 cm

Solution ....

4 Check your answer. Show your work.

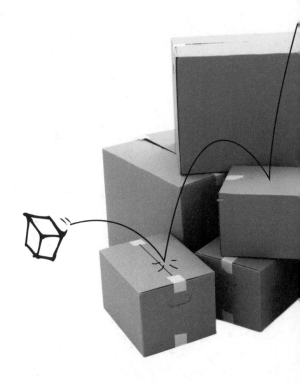

    ©Curriculum Associates, LLC   Copying is not permitted

Develop Finding Volume Using Unit Cubes

21

Read and try to solve the problem below.

> Abigail uses cardboard to build a rectangular prism like the one shown below. What is the volume of the prism?
>
>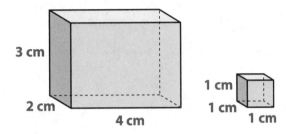

TRY IT

 **Math Toolkit**

- unit cubes
- 1-cm grid paper
- isometric dot paper

DISCUSS IT

Ask your partner: Why did you choose that strategy?

Tell your partner: I knew . . . so I . . .

©Curriculum Associates, LLC   Copying is not permitted

Explore different ways to understand finding the volume of a rectangular prism.

> **Abigail uses cardboard to build a rectangular prism like the one shown below. What is the volume of the prism?**

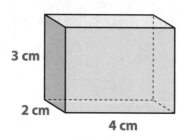

3 cm
2 cm
4 cm

1 cm
1 cm
1 cm

PICTURE IT

You can find the volume of the prism by filling it with unit cubes and counting the number of cubes.

Use unit cubes that are each 1 cubic centimeter.

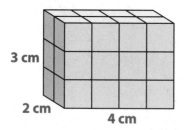

3 cm
2 cm
4 cm

MODEL IT

You can also find the volume by counting the number of cubes in one layer and the number of layers.

Use unit cubes that are each 1 cubic centimeter.

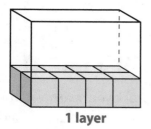 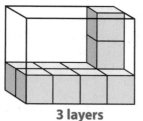

1 layer   3 layers

©Curriculum Associates, LLC   Copying is not permitted

CONNECT IT
Now you will use the problem from the previous page to help you understand how to find the volume of a rectangular prism.

1 Look at the model in **Picture It** on the previous page. Count the number of cubes in one layer. There are .... cubes in one layer.

2 How could you find the number of cubes in one layer without counting the cubes?

3 Once you know how many cubes are in one layer, what else do you need to know to find the volume?

4 There are 8 cubes in each layer and there are 3 layers. What multiplication expression can you write to find the volume of the prism? ....

5 What is the volume of Abigail's rectangular prism? ....

6 Explain how you can use multiplication to find the volume of a rectangular prism.

7 REFLECT

Look back at your **Try It**, strategies by classmates, and **Picture It** and **Model It**. Which models or strategies do you like best for finding the volume of a rectangular prism? Explain.

....

....

....

....

....

APPLY IT

Use what you just learned to solve these problems.

8 What is the volume of the rectangular prism at the right? Show your work.

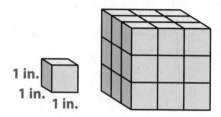

Solution ....

9 Mr. Wong finds the volume of a box by filling it with 1-foot unit cubes, as shown below. What is the volume of Mr. Wong's box? Show your work.

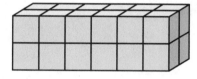

Solution ....

10 Jamila wants to find the volume of the rectangular box at the right. What is the volume of the box?

Ⓐ 18 cubic units

Ⓑ 30 cubic centimeters

Ⓒ 36 cubic centimeters

Ⓓ 36 cubic inches

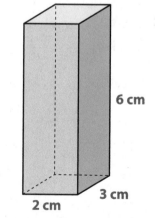

©Curriculum Associates, LLC Copying is not permitted

Practice Finding Volume Using Unit Cubes

Study the Example showing how to use layers to find the volume of a rectangular prism. Then solve problems 1–7.

EXAMPLE

Keith uses this box to store his colored markers. What is the volume of the box?

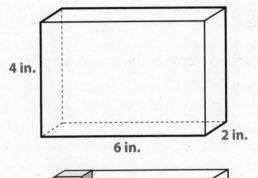

Think about filling the box with 1-inch cubes. One layer has 2 rows of 6 cubes, or 12 cubes. There are 4 layers of cubes.

$$12 + 12 + 12 + 12 = 48, \text{ or } 12 \times 4 = 48$$

The volume of the box is 48 cubic inches.

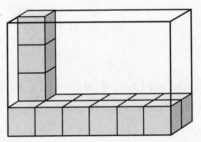

1 Prism G is filled with unit cubes that have side length 1 centimeter.

There are .... layers with .... cubes in each layer.

.... cubes + ... cubes = ... cubes

The volume is ....

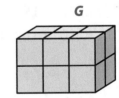

2 Prism H is filled with unit cubes that have side length 1 foot.

There are .... layers with .... cubes in each layer.

.... × .... cubes = ... cubes

The volume is ....

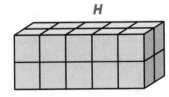

©Curriculum Associates, LLC   Copying is not permitted

3 What is the volume of the rectangular prism at the right? Show your work.

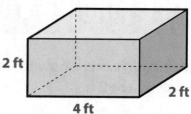

2 ft

2 ft

4 ft

Solution

4 What is the volume of the box at the right? Show your work.

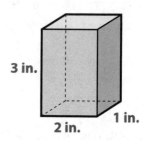

3 in.

1 in.

2 in.

Solution

5 A box is 2 inches long, 1 inch wide, and 6 inches tall. What is the relationship between the volume of this box and the one in problem 4? Tell how you know.

6 Box *D* and Box *E* are made from unit cubes of the same size. Which has a greater volume, Box *D* or Box *E*? Explain.

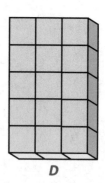

D

7 Add a layer to Box *D* and compare the volume of the new Box *D* to the volume of Box *E*.

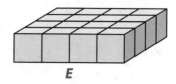

E

©Curriculum Associates, LLC   Copying is not permitted

Refine Finding Volume Using Unit Cubes

Complete the Example below. Then solve problems 1–9.

EXAMPLE

Pedro has a storage box with a volume of 36 cubic feet. He knows that the box is 4 feet long and 3 feet wide. How high is the box?

Look at how you could show your work using a drawing and multiplication facts.

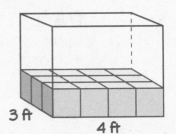

3 ft
4 ft

$3 \times 4 = 12$

$12 \times \square = 36$

$12 \times 3 = 36$

Solution ....

The student started by finding the number of cubes in the bottom layer.

PAIR/SHARE
Could you solve this problem another way?

APPLY IT

1 A box measures 6 centimeters long, 2 centimeters wide, and 4 centimeters high. What is the volume of the box? Show your work.

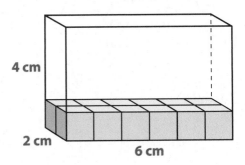

4 cm

2 cm
6 cm

How many layers of cubes will there be in the box?

PAIR/SHARE
Can you use multiplication to solve this problem?

Solution ....

2 Kamala made the figure below using cubes. What is the volume of Kamala's figure? Show your work.

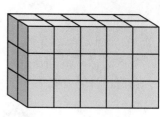

How many cubes are there in each layer?

1 in.
1 in.
1 in.

PAIR/SHARE
How did you decide which method to use to solve the problem?

Solution ....

3 What is the volume of the rectangular prism below?

1 ft
1 ft 1 ft

There is more than one way to find the volume of a rectangular prism.

Ⓐ 6 square feet

Ⓑ 6 cubic feet

Ⓒ 8 square feet

Ⓓ 8 cubic feet

Nam chose Ⓓ as the correct answer. How did he get that answer?

PAIR/SHARE
Does Nam's answer make sense?

  ©Curriculum Associates, LLC   Copying is not permitted

4 How many 1-centimeter unit cubes are in the bottom layer of the rectangular prism at the right?

Ⓐ 3

Ⓑ 6

Ⓒ 12

Ⓓ 24

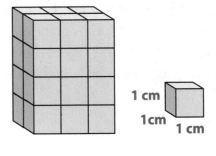

5 Which expressions can be used to find the volume, in cubic feet, of the rectangular prism at the right?

Ⓐ 30 × 4

Ⓑ (5 + 6) × 4

Ⓒ 30 + 30 + 30 + 30

Ⓓ 5 + 6 + 4

Ⓔ 30 + 4

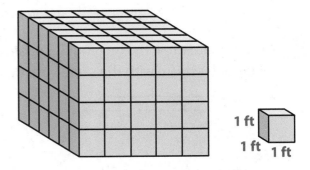

6 Flora has a rectangular gift box that has a volume of 24 cubic inches. The box is 2 inches tall. Determine if the gift box could have the given length and width.

	Yes	No
Length: 11 inches; Width: 11 inches	Ⓐ	Ⓑ
Length: 4 inches; Width: 3 inches	Ⓒ	Ⓓ
Length: 2 inches; Width: 10 inches	Ⓔ	Ⓕ
Length: 6 inches; Width: 2 inches	Ⓖ	Ⓗ
Length: 1 inch; Width: 12 inches	Ⓘ	Ⓙ

7 Both figures are filled with unit cubes of the same size. Which rectangular prism has the greater volume, Figure *A* or Figure *B*? Show your work.

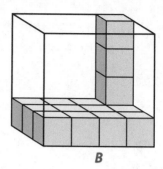
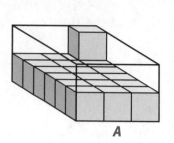

A   B

.... has the greater volume.

8 **Part A** Mato drew the rectangular prism shown below. Draw and label a different rectangular prism with the same volume as Mato's prism.

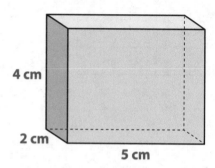

4 cm

2 cm

5 cm

Part B Explain how you know that the volume of your prism is the same as the volume of Mato's prism.

9 MATH JOURNAL

Jorge uses 1-centimeter cubes to make a rectangular prism. Each layer of his prism is 2 cubes long and 5 cubes wide. His prism has 6 layers. Explain two ways to find the volume of Jorge's prism.

☑ SELF CHECK Go back to the Unit 1 Opener and see what you can check off.

Find Volume Using Formulas

Dear Family,

This week your child is learning to find the volume of a solid figure using a formula.

You can use a formula to find the volume of a rectangular prism if you know its length, width, and height. The picture shows a gift bag that is 4 inches long, 2 inches wide, and 3 inches high. The model beside the bag shows the number of 1-inch cubes that would fill the bag.

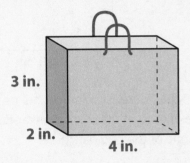
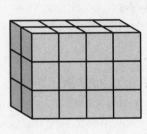

Using the model, you can find the volume of the cube by multiplying the number of cubes in each layer by the number of layers.

The equation to the right shows that multiplying the number of cubes in each layer by the number of layers is the same as multiplying length, width, and height. This is one of the volume formulas your child is learning to use.

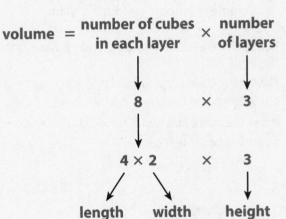

Volume = length × width × height
Volume = 4 inches × 2 inches × 3 inches
    = (8 × 3) cubic inches
    = 24 cubic inches

The volume of the gift bag is 24 cubic inches.

Invite your child to share what he or she knows about finding volume using a formula by doing the following activity together.

©Curriculum Associates, LLC   Copying is not permitted

ACTIVITY USE A VOLUME FORMULA

Do this activity with your child to find volume using a formula.

Work with your child to use a formula to find the volume of the L-shaped solid figure shown at the right.

- The figure is composed of two rectangular prisms. Ask your child to talk about different ways to break the figure apart into two smaller rectangular prisms.

- Choose two ways to break the figure into rectangular prisms. Have your child draw pictures of the two ways to break up the figure and label the lengths, widths, and heights.

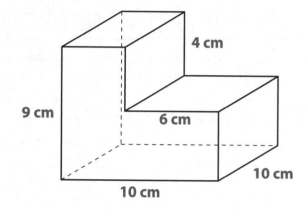

- Start with one of the ways your child broke up the figure. Have him or her use the volume formula below to find the volume of each of the smaller rectangular prisms. Then add the volumes to find the volume of the original figure.

    Volume = length × width × height

- Repeat for the other way your child broke up the figure.

- Have your child compare the two volumes he or she found for the figure. They should be the same. Ask your child: *Suppose there were a third way to break the figure into two other rectangular prisms. Would the volume of the figure be the same?* (Yes.)

©Curriculum Associates, LLC   Copying is not permitted

Explore Finding Volume Using Formulas

Previously, you learned how to find volume by counting unit cubes and by using addition and multiplication strategies. Now you will learn how to find volume using a formula. Use what you know to try to solve the problem below.

> Becky uses 1-inch cubes to create a model for a small paper gift bag she is making. Her model is a rectangular prism. What is the volume of Becky's model?

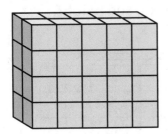

1 in.
1 in. 1 in.

Florida Standards

5.MD.3.5b Apply the formulas $V = l \times w \times h$ and $V = B \times h$ for rectangular prisms to find volumes of right rectangular prisms with whole-number edge lengths in the context of solving real world and mathematical problems.

5.MD.3.5c Recognize volume as additive. Find volumes of solid figures composed of two non-overlapping right rectangular prisms by adding the volumes of the non-overlapping parts, applying this technique to solve real world problems.

5.MD.3.5a

TRY IT

Math Toolkit
- unit cubes
- grid paper
- isometric dot paper

DISCUSS IT

Ask your partner: Do you agree with me? Why or why not?

Tell your partner: I agree with you about . . . because . . .

©Curriculum Associates, LLC   Copying is not permitted

CONNECT IT

1 LOOK BACK

Explain how you can find the volume of Becky's model without counting each cube.

2 LOOK AHEAD

Becky's finished gift bag is shown below. You can find the volume with a formula. Use the letters ℓ, w, and h to represent the **length**, **width**, and **height**.

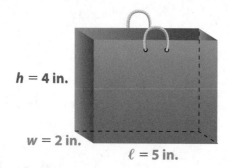
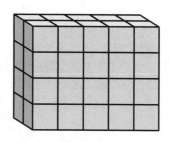

$h = 4$ in.

$w = 2$ in.

$\ell = 5$ in.

a. The bottom of a rectangular prism can be called its **base**. The letter **B** is used to represent the **area of the base**.

Write an equation using the area of the base to find the bag's volume **V**. Then complete the formula with a letter.

$$\text{.............} = \text{.............} \times \text{.............}$$
$$V \quad = \quad B \quad \times \text{.............}$$

b. Use the letters shown in the formula below to help you complete another equation for the volume of the bag. Then complete the formula.

$$\text{.............} = \text{.............} \times \text{.............} \times \text{.............}$$
$$V \quad = \quad \ell \quad \times \quad w \quad \times \text{.............}$$

3 REFLECT

How are the two volume formulas you wrote above alike? How are they different?

....

....

....

Prepare for Finding Volume Using Formulas

1 Think about what you know about formulas. Fill in each box. Use words, numbers, and pictures. Show as many ideas as you can.

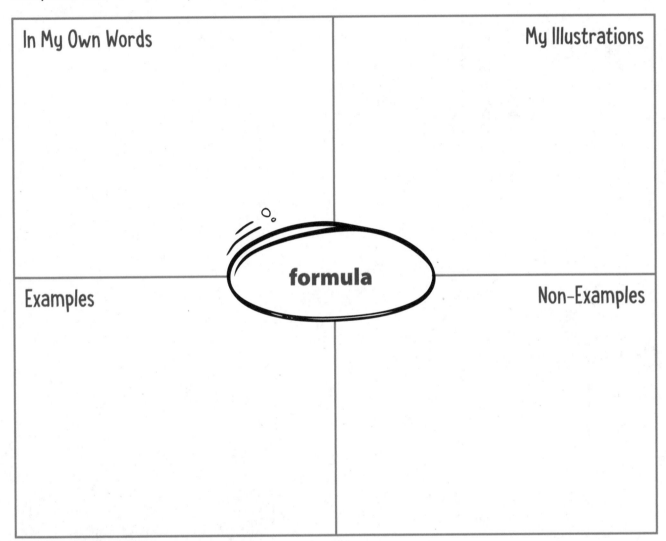

In My Own Words	My Illustrations

formula

Examples	Non-Examples

2 Find the volume of the rectangular prism. Explain.

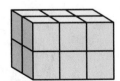

1 unit cube

©Curriculum Associates, LLC   Copying is not permitted

3 Solve the problem. Show your work.

Adrien uses 1-inch cubes to create a model for a small box he is making. His model is a rectangular prism. What is the volume of Adrien's model?

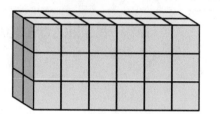

1 in.
1 in. 1 in.

Solution ....

4 Check your answer. Show your work.

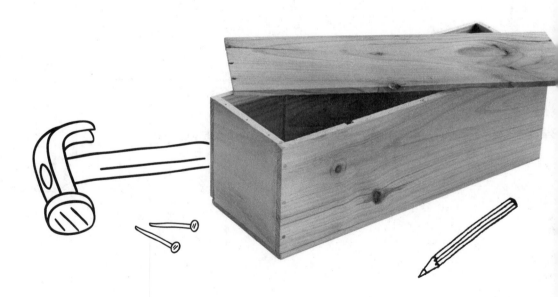

   ©Curriculum Associates, LLC   Copying is not permitted

Develop Finding Volume Using Formulas

Read and try to solve the problem below.

> Gareth has a rectangular pencil cup on his desk. The cup is 3 inches long, 2 inches wide, and 5 inches high. What is the volume of the pencil cup?

TRY IT

 **Math Toolkit**

- unit cubes
- grid paper
- isometric dot paper

DISCUSS IT

Ask your partner: Why did you choose that strategy?

Tell your partner: I knew . . . so I . . .

©Curriculum Associates, LLC   Copying is not permitted

Explore different ways to understand using the dimensions of a rectangular prism to find its volume.

> Gareth has a rectangular pencil cup on his desk. The cup is 3 inches long, 2 inches wide, and 5 inches high. What is the volume of the pencil cup?

PICTURE IT

You can picture the pencil cup as a rectangular prism made up of 1-inch cubes.

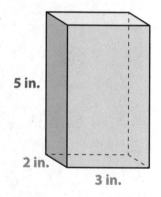

MODEL IT

You can draw a model of the pencil cup and label its dimensions. Then use a volume formula.

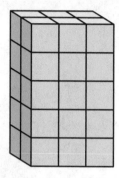

5 in.

2 in.

3 in.

$V = \ell \times w \times h$ or $V = B \times h$

   ©Curriculum Associates, LLC   Copying is not permitted

CONNECT IT

Now you will use the problem from the previous page to help you understand and use formulas to find volume.

1 Explain how you can find the volume of the pencil cup using the prism shown in **Picture It**. Find the volume.

2 Explain how the area of the base of the prism shown in **Model It** relates to the prism in **Picture It**.

3 Explain how you can use the prism in **Model It** to find the volume of the pencil cup.

4 Use the volume formulas shown in **Model It** to write two different multiplication equations you can use to find the volume of the pencil cup.

5 Explain how you can use the dimensions of a rectangular prism to find its volume.

6 REFLECT

Look back at your **Try It**, strategies by classmates, and **Picture It** and **Model It**. Which models or strategies do you like best for using the dimensions of a rectangular prism to find its volume? Explain.

....

....

....

....

©Curriculum Associates, LLC   Copying is not permitted

APPLY IT

Use what you just learned to solve these problems.

7 What is the volume of a rectangular jewelry box with a length of 8 centimeters, a width of 5 centimeters, and a height of 4 centimeters? Show your work.

Solution ....

8 How much space is taken up by a book that is 12 inches long, 10 inches wide, and 1 inch tall? Show your work.

Solution ....

9 A rectangular prism has a volume of 100 cubic meters. One of the dimensions is 5 meters. Which pairs of measurements could be the other two dimensions of the prism?

Ⓐ 1 meter, 20 meters

Ⓑ 5 meters, 10 meters

Ⓒ 10 meters, 10 meters

Ⓓ 4 meters, 5 meters

Ⓔ 20 meters, 20 meters

©Curriculum Associates, LLC   Copying is not permitted

Practice Finding Volume Using Formulas

**Study the Example showing how to use formulas to find the volume of
a rectangular prism. Then solve problems 1–7.**

EXAMPLE

Gwen puts her leftover food in a rectangular container. The container is 6 inches
long, 5 inches wide, and 2 inches tall. What is the volume of the container?

Use the formula *volume = length × width × height*.

$V = \ell \times w \times h = 6 \times 5 \times 2$, or 60 cubic inches

Or use the formula *volume = area of the base × height*.
The *area of the base* is the same as the *length × width*.

$B = 6 \times 5$, or **30**

$V = B \times h = 30 \times 2$, or 60 cubic inches

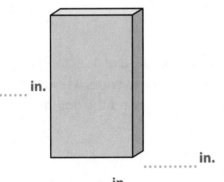

1 Ted's box is 4 inches tall, 3 inches long, and 1 inch wide.

   a. Label the picture of the box with its dimensions.

   b. What is the volume of the box? Show your work.

   in.

   in.

Solution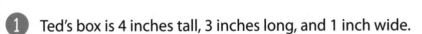

   in.

2 A rectangular prism has a square base with sides that are 2 feet long. The height of
the prism is 5 feet. What is the volume of the prism? Show your work.

Solution ....

3   Elon's shed is 10 feet long, 6 feet wide, and 8 feet tall.
    What is the volume of the shed? Show your work.

Solution ....

4   The base of a rectangular prism has a length of 2 centimeters and has
    a width of 4 centimeters. The height of the prism is 3 centimeters.
    What is the volume of the prism? Show your work.

Solution ....

5   What is the volume of a box that is 8 inches long, 2 inches wide, and
    6 inches tall? Show your work.

Solution ....

6   The base of a rectangular prism is a rectangle that is 7 inches long and
    5 inches wide. Its height is 10 inches. Write two different equations that you can
    use to find the volume.

7   Jin has two boxes. Box *A* has dimensions of 6 centimeters, 5 centimeters, and
    9 centimeters. Box *B* has dimensions of 4 centimeters, 10 centimeters, and
    7 centimeters. Which box holds more? Explain.

Develop Breaking Apart Figures to Find Volume

Read and try to solve the problem below.

Bethany has a raised garden bed. The diagram shows its measurements. All the corners are right angles. If she fills the bed to the top with soil, how many cubic feet of soil will Bethany need?

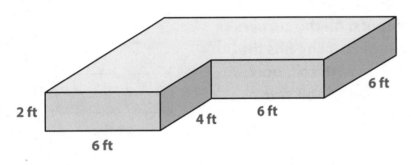

TRY IT

 Math Toolkit

- unit cubes
- grid paper
- isometric dot paper

DISCUSS IT

Ask your partner: Can you explain that again?

Tell your partner: I knew . . . so I . . .

©Curriculum Associates, LLC　Copying is not permitted

Explore different ways to understand finding the volume of a solid figure by breaking it apart into two rectangular prisms.

Bethany has a raised garden bed. The diagram shows its measurements. All the corners are right angles. If she fills the bed to the top with soil, how many cubic feet of soil will Bethany need?

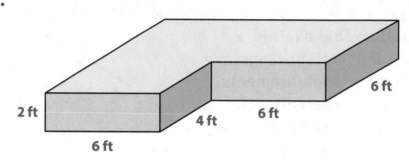

MODEL IT

You can break the garden bed into two rectangular prisms this way.

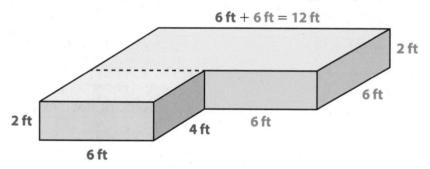

One rectangular prism measures **6 feet × 4 feet × 2 feet**.
The other rectangular prism measures **12 feet × 6 feet × 2 feet**.

MODEL IT

You can also break the garden bed into two rectangular prisms in a different way.

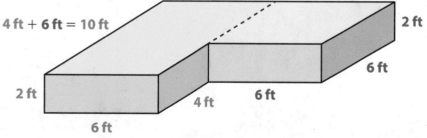

One rectangular prism measures **6 feet × 10 feet × 2 feet**.
The other rectangular prism measures **6 feet × 6 feet × 2 feet**.

©Curriculum Associates, LLC   Copying is not permitted

CONNECT IT

Now you will use the problem from the previous page to help you understand ways to break apart a solid figure to find its volume.

1 Look at the first **Model It**. How can you find the volume of each rectangular prism?

2 How can you find the volume of the entire garden bed?

3 What is the volume of the entire garden bed? Show your work. ....

4 Now look at the second **Model It**. Show how to find the volume of the garden bed if you break it apart this way.

5 Do you need to break apart a solid figure in a certain way to find its volume? Use the problem from the previous page to explain your reasoning.

6 **REFLECT**

Look back at your **Try It**, strategies by classmates, and **Model Its**. Which models or strategies do you like best for breaking apart solid figures to find volume? Explain.

....

....

....

....

....

....

APPLY IT

Use what you just learned to solve these problems.

7 The Recreation Center has an L-shaped pool. One part of the pool is 8 meters by 6 meters. The other part is 12 meters by 6 meters. The whole pool is 4 meters deep. What is the volume of the entire pool? Show your work.

Solution ....

8 What is the volume of the solid figure below? Show your work.

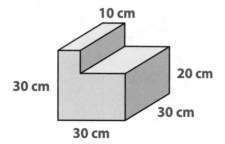

Solution ....

9 What is the volume of the solid figure below? Show your work.

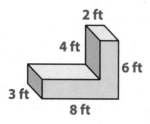

Solution ....

©Curriculum Associates, LLC   Copying is not permitted

Practice Breaking Apart Figures to Find Volume

Study the Example showing how to break apart a solid figure into rectangular prisms and find its volume. Then solve problems 1–8.

EXAMPLE

Molly wants to know how much soil she needs to fill her two-tiered planter, shown below. What is the volume of the planter?

You can break the figure into two rectangular prisms in different ways.

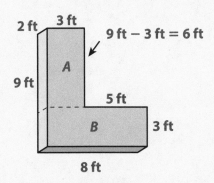

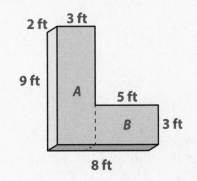

Prism A measures 3 ft × 6 ft × 2 ft.
Volume of Prism A = 36 cubic feet

Prism B measures 8 ft × 3 ft × 2 ft.
Volume of Prism B = 48 cubic feet

Volume of planter = 36 + 48, or 84
The volume is 84 cubic feet.

Prism A measures 3 ft × 9 ft × 2 ft.
Volume of Prism A = 54 cubic feet

Prism B measures 5 ft × 3 ft × 2 ft.
Volume of Prism B = 30 cubic feet

Volume of planter = 54 + 30, or 84
The volume is 84 cubic feet.

1 Show how to find the volume of Prism D.

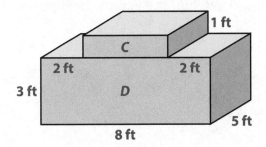

2 Find the volume of Prism C.

3 What is the volume of the whole figure?

④ Draw lines in Figures *A* and *B* to separate them into two rectangular prisms. Do each in a different way.

⑤ Show how to find the volume of Figure *A*.

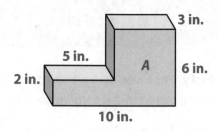

⑥ Show how to find the volume of Figure *B*.

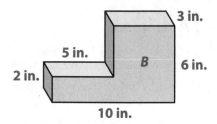

⑦ What is the volume of Figure *X*? Show your work.

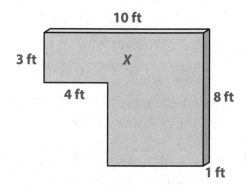

Solution ....

⑧ Show how to break Figure *S* into three rectangular prisms. Then find the volume of Figure *S*. Show your work.

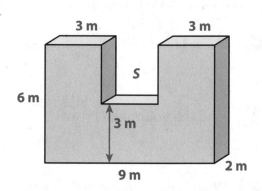

Solution ....

 ©Curriculum Associates, LLC Copying is not permitted

Refine Finding Volume Using Formulas

Complete the Example below. Then solve problems 1–9.

EXAMPLE

Coen is making a clay vase. He wants the interior of the vase to be a rectangular prism with base 3 inches long and 3 inches wide. He wants the vase to hold 45 cubic inches of water. How tall should Coen make the vase?

Look at how you could use a formula to solve the problem.

$$\text{Volume} = \ell \times w \times h$$
$$45 = 3 \times 3 \times h$$
$$45 = 9 \times h$$
$$45 \div 9 = h$$
$$5 = h$$

Solution ....

The student wrote an equation using the formula for volume. The height is the unknown.

PAIR/SHARE
Did you and your partner solve the problem the same way?

APPLY IT

1 The diagram shows the dimensions of a cement walkway, where all of the sides meet at right angles. What is the total volume of cement needed to make the walkway? Show your work.

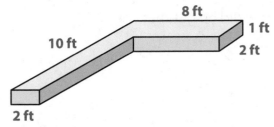

After you break apart the figure, how will you find the missing measurements?

PAIR/SHARE
How did you and your partner decide how to break apart the solid figure?

Solution ....

©Curriculum Associates, LLC   Copying is not permitted

2 The rectangular prism shown below has a volume of 42 cubic meters. What is the length of the prism? Show your work.

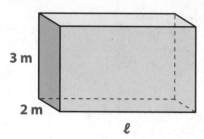

What dimensions are labeled on the prism?

Solution ....

PAIR/SHARE
How could you check your answer?

3 A cube is a rectangular prism whose side lengths are all the same. What is the volume of a cube with a side length of 2 feet?

Ⓐ 4 cubic feet

Ⓑ 6 cubic feet

Ⓒ 8 cubic feet

Ⓓ 12 cubic feet

Danny chose Ⓑ as the correct answer. How did he get that answer?

Each side of a cube is a square.

PAIR/SHARE
Does Danny's answer make sense?

©Curriculum Associates, LLC   Copying is not permitted

4 A rectangular prism has a square base with side lengths of 5 centimeters and a height of 7 centimeters. What is the volume of the prism?

Ⓐ 35 cubic centimeters

Ⓑ 140 cubic centimeters

Ⓒ 175 cubic centimeters

Ⓓ 245 cubic centimeters

5 The diagram below shows the measurements of a mold used to make sandcastles. Which expressions can be used to find the volume of the mold, in cubic inches?

Ⓐ $(2 \times 5 \times 3) + (5 \times 5 \times 3)$

Ⓑ $(2 \times 5 \times 3) + (7 \times 5 \times 3)$

Ⓒ $(2 \times 5 \times 6) + (5 \times 5 \times 3)$

Ⓓ $(2 \times 5 \times 6) + (7 \times 5 \times 3)$

Ⓔ $(2 \times 5 \times 3) + (7 \times 5 \times 6)$

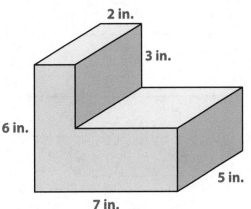

6 The diagram shows the dimensions of two identical rectangular prisms joined together. What is the combined volume, in cubic meters, of the two prisms?

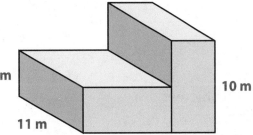

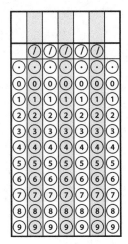

©Curriculum Associates, LLC   Copying is not permitted

7 A cardboard box has a volume of 60 cubic feet. Give three different sets of measurements that could be the dimensions of the box.

.... feet × .... feet × .... feet

.... feet × .... feet × .... feet

.... feet × .... feet × .... feet

8 Rami designed a small pond for a restaurant. The diagram below shows the measurements of the pond. How many cubic feet of water are needed to fill the pond? Show your work.

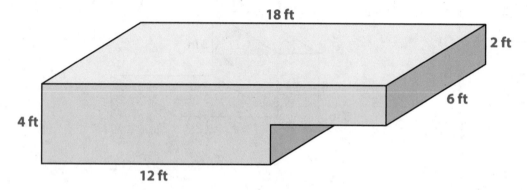

18 ft

2 ft

6 ft

4 ft

12 ft

.... cubic feet

9 MATH JOURNAL

Describe a real-world object that can be modeled by a rectangular prism and give its dimensions. Use a formula to find the volume of the object.

✓ SELF CHECK Go back to the Unit 1 Opener and see what you can check off.

Multiply Whole Numbers

Dear Family,

This week your child is learning to multiply multi-digit numbers.

One way to find 124 × 25 is to set up the problem vertically to find partial products that can be added to find the total product.

First, multiply each digit in 124 by the 5 ones in 25.

```
    124
  ×   5
     20
    100
  + 500
    620
```

Then multiply each digit in 124 by the 2 tens in 25.

```
    124
  ×  20
     80
    400
 + 2,000
   2,480
```

partial product

Lastly, add the partial products to find the product: 124 × 25 = **620** + **2,480** = **3,100**.

Partial products are the basis of the standard algorithm for multiplying multi-digit numbers. An **algorithm** is a set of routine steps used to solve problems.

Your child is learning how to record the steps of the standard algorithm in a condensed format, with regrouping shown above the problem.

Notice how the partial products appear as steps in the standard algorithm.

```
      124                  ¹²
    ×  25                 124
       20              ×   25
      100                 620
      500            + 2,480
       80               3,100
      400
  + 2,000
    3,100
```

Another way your child is learning to multiply is with an area model, which gives a visual representation of the multiplication.

Invite your child to share what he or she knows about multiplying multi-digit numbers by doing the following activity together.

ACTIVITY MULTIPLY WHOLE NUMBERS

Do this activity with your child to multiply whole numbers.

Materials magazine or newspaper

Work with your child to find a real-life example of using multiplication that involves the number of words in a magazine or newspaper article.

Sometimes a reporter has to write a story with a certain number of words, for example, 500 words. Multiplication is a good way to find the number of words in a story.

- Have your child choose an article from a magazine or newspaper.

- Ask your child to count the number of words in one paragraph and record the number on a sheet of paper.

- Then count the number of paragraphs in the article.

- Ask your child: *Suppose each paragraph had the same number of words. How could you find how many words are in the article? How many words are in the article?* (Multiply the number of words in a paragraph by the number of paragraphs.)

- Then ask your child: *If each paragraph has a different number of words, is the answer to the previous question an exact answer or an estimate for the total number of words in the article?* (It is an estimate because the number of words in each paragraph varies.)

EXPLORING MARS

Have you ever thought about exploring Mars? Even if you haven't, other people certainly have. Mars was first explored by telescope in the 1700s. Early astronomers observed ice caps, dust clouds, and dark streaks. They wondered if there could be life on Mars.

In modern times, the United States, the former Soviet Union, and other countries have sent spacecraft to gather more information about the "red planet." The first missions to Mars flew near the planet. In November 1964, the U.S. National Aeronautics and Space Administration (NASA) launched Mariner 4. This spacecraft flew past Mars in July 1965 and took the first close-up photographs. The pictures were blurry, but they helped scientists learn what Mars looked like. Then new technology allowed the United States to get even closer. In 1975, NASA launched Viking 1 and Viking 2. Viking 1 landed on the surface of Mars on July 19, 1976. Viking 2 followed on September 3, 1976. Both Viking 2 explored differe...

The Viking 2 spacecraft took this photograph of the Martian surface in 1976. Mars is red because its surface is made of iron oxide, also known as rust.

NASA also built space rovers that could is a solar-powered vehicle that is operated fr NASA spacecraft have carried rovers to Mars. landed the first Mars rover, Sojourner, in 199 photographs back to Earth and collected soil

Two more rovers were launched in 2003. rovers Spirit and Opportunity discovered evi lost contact with Spirit in 2010. But, as of April collecting data.

Finally, on November 26, 2011, NASA laur named Curiosity. Since landing in 2012, this M planet has ever been able to support life. Curio rocks and soil.

Over the past 50 years, scientists have lear For example, they have a better understanding its atmosphere. With future missions, they hope red planet.

 ©Curriculum Associates, LLC   Copying is not permitted

Explore Multiplying Whole Numbers

Florida Standards

5.NBT.2.5 Fluently multiply multi-digit whole numbers using the standard algorithm.

You know how to multiply a two-digit number by a two-digit number. Now you will multiply greater multi-digit numbers. Use what you know to try to solve the problem below.

A mall has a rectangular outdoor space that is 127 feet by 46 feet. There is a grassy section with a width of 40 feet and a cement sidewalk with a width of 6 feet. What is the area of the outdoor space in square feet?

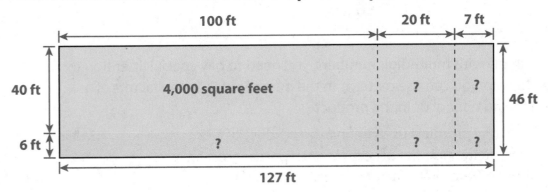

TRY IT

 Math Toolkit

- base-ten blocks
- base-ten grid paper
- grid paper
- index cards

DISCUSS IT

Ask your partner: Can you explain that again?

Tell your partner: The strategy I used to find the answer was . . .

©Curriculum Associates, LLC   Copying is not permitted

CONNECT IT

1 LOOK BACK

The area of the outdoor space is 127×46. How can you find this product?

2 LOOK AHEAD

When you multiply with multi-digit numbers, you need to pay special attention to place value. To help, you can use patterns in the number of 0s in the factors of a product and the number of 0s in the product.

a. Look at the partial products used to find the product of 512 and 24. Compare the number of zeros in each partial product to the number of zeros in its factors. Look at both red and blue zeros. Describe any patterns you see.

$$
\begin{array}{r}
512 \\
\times \quad 24 \\
\hline
8 \longrightarrow 4 \times 2 \\
40 \longrightarrow 4 \times 10 \\
2{,}000 \longrightarrow 4 \times 500 \\
40 \longrightarrow 20 \times 2 \\
200 \longrightarrow 20 \times 10 \\
+\ 10{,}000 \longrightarrow 20 \times 500 \\
\hline
12{,}288
\end{array}
$$

b. Explain why the partial product 4×500 has three 0s, not just two 0s.

3 REFLECT

Why is it important to pay attention to place value when multiplying multi-digit numbers?

....

....

....

....

©Curriculum Associates, LLC   Copying is not permitted

Prepare for Multiplying Whole Numbers

1 Think about what you know about multiplying multi-digit whole numbers. Fill in each box. Use words, numbers, and pictures. Show as many ideas as you can.

What Is It?	What I Know About It

partial products

Examples	Examples	Examples

2 Zula multiplied 761 by 5 using partial products. Is she correct? Explain.

```
      761
  ×     5
        5
       30
 + 3,500
    3,535
```

③ Solve the problem. Show your work.

A city has a rectangular park that is 143 feet by 32 feet. There is a grassy field with a width of 30 feet. Next to the field there is a flower bed with a width of 2 feet. What is the area of the park in square feet?

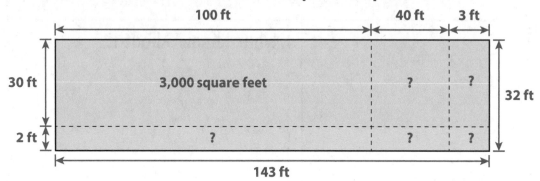

Solution ....

④ Check your answer. Show your work.

  ©Curriculum Associates, LLC   Copying is not permitted

Develop Multiplying Multi-Digit Whole Numbers

Read and try to solve the problem below.

> There are 128 pens in a full box. How many
> pens are in 35 full boxes?

TRY IT

 **Math Toolkit**

- base-ten blocks
- base-ten grid paper
- grid paper
- index cards

DISCUSS IT

Ask your partner: Why did you choose that strategy?

Tell your partner:
I knew . . . so I . . .

©Curriculum Associates, LLC   Copying is not permitted

Explore different ways to understand multiplying multi-digit whole numbers.

There are 128 pens in a full box. How many pens are in 35 full boxes?

MODEL IT
Use an area model to show partial products.

To find the product 128×35, sketch a rectangle with dimensions 128 by 35.

128 is **100 + 20 + 8**.

35 is **30 + 5**.

	100	+	20	+	8
30	$30 \times 100 = \mathbf{3{,}000}$		$30 \times 20 = \mathbf{600}$		$30 \times 8 = \mathbf{240}$
+ 5	$5 \times 100 = \mathbf{500}$		$5 \times 20 = \mathbf{100}$		$5 \times 8 = \mathbf{40}$

First row: $3{,}000 + 600 + 240 = 3{,}840$

Second row: $500 + 100 + 40 = 640$

MODEL IT
Use the distributive property to find partial products and add them.

$128 \times 35 = 128 \times (30 + 5)$

$128 \times (30 + 5) = (128 \times 30) + (128 \times 5)$

$$
\begin{array}{r}
128 \\
\times \quad 30 \\
\hline
240 \longrightarrow 30 \times 8 \\
600 \longrightarrow 30 \times 20 \\
+\ 3{,}000 \longrightarrow 30 \times 100 \\
\hline
3{,}840
\end{array}
\qquad
\begin{array}{r}
128 \\
\times \quad 5 \\
\hline
40 \longrightarrow 5 \times 8 \\
100 \longrightarrow 5 \times 20 \\
+\ 500 \longrightarrow 5 \times 100 \\
\hline
640
\end{array}
$$

©Curriculum Associates, LLC   Copying is not permitted

CONNECT IT
Now you will use the problem from the previous page to help you understand how to multiply multi-digit whole numbers.

1 Why is the area model divided into six sections?

2 How do the three partial products in each multiplication equation in the second **Model It** relate to the three sections in each row of the area model?

3 Use the partial products 3,840 and 640 to find the product 128 $\times$ 35. How many pens are in 35 full boxes?

4 Would the product change if 30 and 5 on the left side of the area model were changed to 20, 10, and 5? Explain.

5 List two different ways you could break up the factors in 239 $\times$ 64 to find the product. Explain why the two ways would have the same product.

6 REFLECT

Look back at your **Try It**, strategies by classmates, and **Model Its**. Which models or strategies do you like best for multiplying multi-digit whole numbers? Explain.

....

....

APPLY IT

Use what you just learned to solve these problems.

7 A library bookshelf holds 156 books. There are 15 bookshelves in a certain section of the library. How many books can the library place on these bookshelves? Show your work.

Solution ....

8 Find the product 405 × 13. Show your work.

Solution ....

9 What is the product of 248 and 11?

Ⓐ 259

Ⓑ 2,480

Ⓒ 2,628

Ⓓ 2,728

©Curriculum Associates, LLC   Copying is not permitted

Practice Multiplying Multi-Digit Whole Numbers

Study the Example showing how to multiply a three-digit number by a two-digit number using the distributive property. Then solve problems 1–3.

EXAMPLE

Find 132×26.

Use the distributive property.

$$132 \times 26 = 132 \times (20 + 6)$$
$$= (132 \times 20) + (132 \times 6)$$

Find the partial products.

```
   132              132
 × 20            ×   6
   40  (20 × 2)     12  (6 × 2)
  600  (20 × 30)   180  (6 × 30)
+ 2,000  (20 × 100)  + 600  (6 × 100)
  2,640            792
```

Write the sum of the partial products. $2,640 + 792 = 3,432$

So, $132 \times 26 = 3,432$.

---

1 Complete the steps to find 253×34.

$253 \times 34 = 253 \times (30 + 4) = ($ .... $\times 30) + ($ .... $\times 4)$

```
        253                          253
    ×   30                       ×     4
        90  (30 × 3)            ..............  (.......... × ..........)
..............  (30 × ..........)   ..............  (.......... × ..........)
+ ..............  (.......... × ..........)   + ..............  (.......... × ..........)
..............                    ..............
```

$253 \times 34 = 7,590 + 1,012 =$ ....

©Curriculum Associates, LLC   Copying is not permitted

2 You can also use an area model to find the product of 253 × 34.

a. Write the missing partial products in the area model.

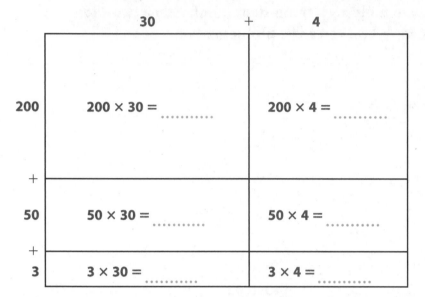

	30	**+**	**4**
200	200 × 30 = ...		200 × 4 = ...
+			
50	50 × 30 = ...		50 × 4 = ...
+			
3	3 × 30 = ...		3 × 4 = ...

b. Write the partial products to complete the equations below.

First column: .... + ... + ... = ...

Second column: .... + ... + ... = ...

c. 253 × 34 = ...

3 Nate's mother drives 225 miles for work each month.
How many miles does she drive for work in 1 year?
(There are 12 months in one year.) Show your work.

Solution ....

   ©Curriculum Associates, LLC   Copying is not permitted

Develop Multiplying with the Standard Algorithm

Read and try to solve the problem below.

Find the product 1,429 × 42.

TRY IT

 Math Toolkit
- base-ten blocks
- base-ten grid paper
- grid paper
- index cards

DISCUSS IT

Ask your partner: Do you agree with me? Why or why not?

Tell your partner: I agree with you about . . . because . . .

Explore different ways to understand how to find a product using the standard algorithm for multiplying multi-digit whole numbers.

Find the product 1,429 × 42.

MODEL IT

You can use partial products.

You can record each partial product in a separate row.

```
        1,429
    ×     42
          18 ⎤
          40 ⎥
         800 ⎥ 2,858
       2,000 ⎦
         360 ⎤
         800 ⎥
      16,000 ⎥ 57,160
    + 40,000 ⎦
```

Now you can add the partial products to find the product.

MODEL IT

You can use the standard algorithm.

An **algorithm** is a set of routine steps used to solve problems. With the standard algorithm for multiplication, you multiply by place value, regrouping and adding as you go. You record all the partial sums for each place value in a single row.

Step 1: Multiply by **ones**. Regroup as needed. Record the partial product in one row.

```
      1
    1,429
  ×   42
    2,858      ◁ partial product
```

Step 2: Multiply by **tens**. Regroup as needed. Record the partial product in a second row.

```
    1 1 3
        1
    1,429
  ×   42
    2,858
  + 57,160    ◁ partial product
```

Now you can add the partial products to find the product.

CONNECT IT

Now you will use the problem from the previous page to help you understand how to connect partial products to the standard algorithm for multiplication.

1 Where do you see multiplying by ones and by tens in the first **Model It**?

2 Look at the second **Model It**. How do the partial products 18, 40, 800, and 2,000 relate to the first step of the standard algorithm model?

3 Look at the second **Model It**. How do the partial products 360, 800, 16,000, and 40,000 relate to the second step of the standard algorithm model?

4 Complete the multiplication in each **Model It** by adding the partial products.

What is 1,429 × 42? ....

5 Compare the partial products model and the standard algorithm model.

6 REFLECT

Look back at your **Try It**, strategies by classmates, and **Model Its**. Which models or strategies do you like best for understanding the standard algorithm for multiplying two multi-digit numbers? Explain.

....

....

....

APPLY IT

Use what you just learned to solve these problems.

7 Find the product 503 × 18. Estimate to check for reasonableness. Show your work.

Solution ....

8 A school supply store has boxes of markers with 25 markers in each box. There are 1,075 boxes of markers in stock. How many markers does the store have in stock? Show your work.

Solution ....

9 What is the product 257 × 34? Use the standard algorithm. Show your work.

Solution ....

©Curriculum Associates, LLC   Copying is not permitted

Practice Multiplying with the Standard Algorithm

Study the Example showing how to multiply multi-digit whole numbers using the standard algorithm. Then solve problems 1–5.

EXAMPLE

Find the product 6,078 × 32 using the standard algorithm.

Find the first partial product (**2** × 6,078).
$$2 \times 8 = 16 \text{ (regroup } \textbf{1 ten)}$$
$$2 \times 70 = 140 + \textbf{10} = 150 \text{ (regroup } \textbf{1 hundred)}$$
$$2 \times 0 = 0 + \textbf{100} = 100$$
$$2 \times 6,000 = 12,000$$
$$12,000 + 100 + 50 + 6 = 12,156$$

$$
\begin{array}{r}
{\scriptstyle 2\,2} \\
{\scriptstyle 1\,1} \\
6,078 \\
\times \quad 32 \\
\hline
12,156 \\
+\ 182,340 \\
\hline
194,496 \\
\end{array}
$$

← partial product
← partial product
← product

Find the second partial product (**30** × 6,078).
$$30 \times 8 = \textbf{240} \text{ (regroup } \textbf{2 hundreds)}$$
$$30 \times 70 = 2,100 + \textbf{200} = \textbf{2,}300 \text{ (regroup } \textbf{2 thousands)}$$
$$30 \times 0 = 0 + \textbf{2,000} = 2,000$$
$$30 \times 6,000 = 180,000$$
$$180,000 + 2,000 + 300 + 40 = 182,340$$

Add the partial products to find the product: 182,340 + 12,156 = 194,496.

1 Which expression shows the numbers that are multiplied to find the partial product 12,060?

$$
\begin{array}{r}
{\scriptstyle 2} \\
1,206 \\
\times \quad 14 \\
\hline
4,824 \\
+\ 12,060 \\
\hline
16,884 \\
\end{array}
$$

Ⓐ 4 × 1,206

Ⓑ 14 × 1,206

Ⓒ 10 × 1,206

Ⓓ 100 × 126

2   Find the product of 512 and 46 using the standard algorithm. Estimate to check for reasonableness. Show your work.

Solution

3   When using the standard algorithm to find the product 5,917 × 29, the first step is multiplying 9 ones by 7 ones. Explain why you regroup before the next step.

$$
\begin{array}{r}
\overset{6}{5,917} \\
\times \quad 29 \\
\hline
3
\end{array}
$$

4   What is the value of the regrouped "1" above the multiplication problem?

Ⓐ 1

Ⓑ 100

Ⓒ 1,000

Ⓓ 10,000

$$
\begin{array}{r}
\overset{2}{}\overset{2}{} \\
\overset{1}{} \\
7,504 \\
\times \quad 52 \\
\hline
15,008 \\
+ \ 375,200 \\
\hline
390,208
\end{array}
$$

5   Find the product 27,405 × 18 using the standard algorithm. Show your work.

Solution

70   **Lesson 4** Multiply Whole Numbers

©Curriculum Associates, LLC   Copying is not permitted

Refine Multiplying Whole Numbers

Complete the Example below. Then solve problems 1–9.

EXAMPLE

Find the product 3,606 × 24.

Look at how you could show your work with the standard algorithm.

$$\begin{array}{r} \overset{1}{}\overset{1}{} \\ \overset{2}{}\overset{2}{} \\ 3,606 \\ \times \quad\quad 24 \\ \hline 14,424 \\ +\ 72,120 \\ \hline 86,544 \end{array}$$

Solution ....

> Why does the product of 3,606 and 2 tens have a 0 in the ones place?

PAIR/SHARE
How are the regrouped ones and hundreds used to find the partial products?

APPLY IT

1. A certain washing machine uses 29 gallons of water for each load of laundry washed. How many gallons of water would the washing machine use for 156 loads of laundry? Show your work.

> What is the role of place value when multiplying two numbers?

PAIR/SHARE
Show and explain how to solve this problem using a different method.

Solution ....

2 Find the product of 1,225 and 45. Use estimation to check the reasonableness of your answer. Show your work.

How could I estimate the answer to this problem?

PAIR/SHARE
Is your answer close to your estimate?

Solution ....

3 Raquel can type 63 words every minute. Rick can type 73 words every minute. How many more words can Rick type than Raquel in 135 minutes?

Ⓐ 1,350

Ⓑ 4,599

Ⓒ 8,505

Ⓓ 9,855

Jared chose Ⓑ as the correct answer. How did he get that answer?

How can I use the difference in the number of words typed by Rick and Raquel every minute to solve this problem?

PAIR/SHARE
Does Jared's answer make sense?

©Curriculum Associates, LLC   Copying is not permitted

4 Mrs. Cady constructs a cube with 216 magnetic blocks. Students in her two classes will each make an identical cube. There are 28 students in one class and 25 students in the other class. How many magnetic blocks does she need for all her students?

Ⓐ 2,160

Ⓑ 5,460

Ⓒ 6,048

Ⓓ 11,448

5 What are the values of the regrouped amounts in the multiplication below?

Ⓐ 3, 2, and 3

Ⓑ 300, 20, and 3

Ⓒ 3,000, 200, and 30

Ⓓ 10,000, 300, and 24

$$
\begin{array}{r}
{}^{3}\,{}^{2}\,{}^{3} \\
1{,}435 \\
\times 17 \\
\hline
10{,}045 \\
+\,14{,}350 \\
\hline
24{,}395
\end{array}
$$

6 Which expressions are equivalent to 179 × 44?

Ⓐ 179 × (4 + 4)

Ⓑ (179 × 40) + (179 × 4)

Ⓒ (100 × 4) + (70 × 4) + (9 × 4)

Ⓓ 4,000 + 2,800 + 360 + 400 + 280 + 36

Ⓔ (100 × 44) + (70 × 44) + (9 × 44)

©Curriculum Associates, LLC   Copying is not permitted

7 Show two different ways to complete the multiplication problem.

$$\begin{array}{r} 3\ \ 1\ \ 4 \\ \times \qquad 5\ \square \\ \hline 1\ \square\ \square\ 6 \end{array} \qquad\qquad \begin{array}{r} 3\ \ 1\ \ 4 \\ \times \qquad 5\ \square \\ \hline 1\ \square\ \square\ 6 \end{array}$$

8 At the start of the day, there are 78 boxes of DVDs in a warehouse. Each box has 116 DVDs. Then 19 of the boxes are shipped. Now how many DVDs are left in the warehouse? Show your work.

.... DVDs

9 MATH JOURNAL

Write a multiplication word problem using a 3-digit number and a 2-digit number. Use the standard algorithm to solve the problem and explain any regrouping that is needed.

☑ SELF CHECK Go back to the Unit 1 Opener and see what you can check off.

Divide Whole Numbers

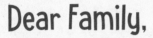

Dear Family,

This week your child is learning to divide whole numbers by a two-digit number.

One way to solve a division problem such as 770 ÷ 14 is to set it up vertically.

First divide the hundreds in 770 by 14.
There are **50** groups of 14 in 700.

Then divide the tens in 770 by 14.
There are **5** groups of 14 in 70.

Add the partial quotients to find the quotient.
    50 + **5** = 55
So, 770 ÷ 14 = 55.

$$
\begin{array}{r}
55 \quad \leftarrow \text{quotient} \\
5 \quad\quad \\
50 \quad \leftarrow \text{partial quotients} \\
14\overline{)770} \\
-700 \\
\hline
70 \\
-70 \\
\hline
0
\end{array}
$$

Another way your child is learning to divide is with an area model, similar to the model used in multiplication.

The area model below shows 770 ÷ 14.

Because multiplication and division are **inverse operations**, or operations that undo each other, use the relationship between them to divide.

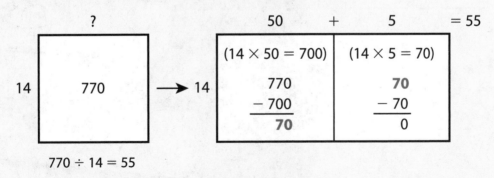

770 ÷ 14 = 55

Both methods result in the same quotient, 55. Notice that 50 and 5 appear as partial quotients in each way of dividing.

Invite your child to share what he or she knows about dividing whole numbers by doing the following activity together.

©Curriculum Associates, LLC   Copying is not permitted **Lesson 5** Divide Whole Numbers **75**

ACTIVITY DIVISION IN THE WORLD

Do this activity with your child to divide whole numbers.

Work with your child to solve real-life problems involving division.

- Choose a favorite book with your child and look at the total number of pages in it. The book should have more than 100 pages. Pick a two-digit number of pages to read each day. Ask: *How many days would it take to read the entire book?*

- Use division to find the answer. For example, suppose the book has 286 pages and the number of pages to be read each day is 15. Divide 286 by 15 to find the number of days it will take to read the book.

- Work together to write and solve the division problem about the book. Encourage your child to use rounding and multiplication to help estimate the quotient first.

- Decide what to do if there is a remainder. Will you read the remaining number of pages on the next day, or will you read the remaining number of pages on the last day of reading?

- Repeat this activity at least 3 more times, either using the same situation or another.

©Curriculum Associates, LLC   Copying is not permitted

Explore Dividing Whole Numbers

You already know how to divide a multi-digit number by a one-digit divisor. Now you will learn how to divide with two-digit divisors. Use what you know to try to solve the problem below.

> There are 264 fifth graders at Wilson Middle School and 12 fifth-grade classrooms. How many students are in each class if each class has the same number of students?

Florida Standards

5.NBT.2.6 Find whole-number quotients of whole numbers with up to four-digit dividends and two-digit divisors, using strategies based on place value, the properties of operations, and/or the relationship between multiplication and division. Illustrate and explain the calculation by using equations, rectangular arrays, and/or area models.

TRY IT

Math Toolkit
- base-ten blocks
- base-ten grid paper
- grid paper
- index cards

DISCUSS IT

Ask your partner: Can you explain that again?

Tell your partner: I started by . . .

CONNECT IT

1 **LOOK BACK**

What is 264 ÷ 12? Explain your reasoning.

2 **LOOK AHEAD**

Multiplication and division are called **inverse operations** because they "undo" each other. For example, the related multiplication and division equations $5 \times 7 = 35$ and $35 \div 5 = 7$ show that if you multiply a number by 5 and then divide the result by 5, you end up with the number you started with.

The multiplication equation related to 264 ÷ 12 = **?** is 12 × **?** = 264.

You can use the related multiplication equation to help you divide.

a. Start by listing products of the divisor, 12, and **multiples of 10**.

Multiple of 10	10	20	30	40	50
12 × Multiple of 10	120				

b. Which row of the table above is related to the dividend in 264 ÷ 12? How could you use the table above to estimate the quotient 264 ÷ 12?

c. Start with 12 × **a multiple of 10** to divide 264 by 12 using an area model. Complete the missing numbers.

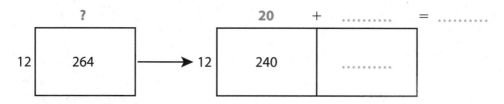

3 **REFLECT**

How can you use the inverse relationship between multiplication and division to check your answer to 264 ÷ 12?

©Curriculum Associates, LLC   Copying is not permitted

Prepare for Dividing Whole Numbers

1   Think about what you know about division. Fill in each box. Use words, numbers, and pictures. Show as many ideas as you can.

Word	In My Own Words	Example
dividend		
divisor		
quotient		

2   Label the *dividend*, *divisor*, and *quotient* of the division equation shown by the area model. Then write the division equation.

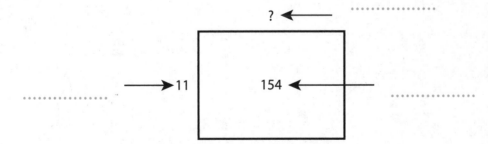

3 Solve the problem. Show your work.

There are 374 fifth graders on a field trip on 11 buses. How many students are on each bus if each bus has the same number of students?

Solution ....

4 Check your answer. Show your work.

©Curriculum Associates, LLC Copying is not permitted

Develop Estimating Quotients

Read and try to solve the problem below.

A toy company packs 504 robots into 21 boxes.
Each box has the same number of robots.
Show how you could estimate the number
of robots in each box.

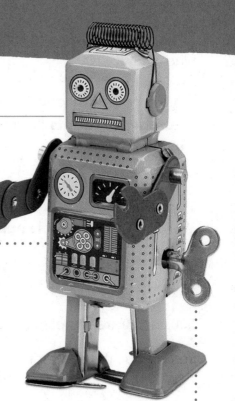

TRY IT

 Math Toolkit
- base-ten blocks
- base-ten grid paper
- grid paper
- index cards

DISCUSS IT

Ask your partner: How did
you get started?

Tell your partner:
I knew . . . so I . . .

©Curriculum Associates, LLC   Copying is not permitted

Explore different ways to understand how to estimate quotients when dividing whole numbers.

> A toy company packs 504 robots into 21 boxes. Each box has the same number of robots. Show how you could estimate the number of robots in each box.

MODEL IT

You can use compatible numbers to estimate a quotient.

Compatible numbers are numbers close to the values of the actual dividend and divisor that allow you to multiply or divide using basic facts.

500 and 20 are compatible numbers that are close to 504 and 21.

You can use them to estimate by thinking $500 \div 20 = ?$ means $20 \times ? = 500$.

?

20	500

MODEL IT

You can use the inverse relationship between multiplication and division to estimate a quotient.

$504 \div 21 = ?$ or $21 \times ? = 504$

Multiply **21** by **multiples of 10**. Make a table.

Number of Robots per Box	Total Number of Robots
10	$21 \times 10 = 210$
20	$21 \times 20 = 420$
30	$21 \times 30 = 630$

    ©Curriculum Associates, LLC   Copying is not permitted

CONNECT IT

Now you will use the problem from the previous page to help you understand how to estimate quotients with two-digit divisors.

1 Look at the first **Model It**. Why are 500 and 20 good choices to use for compatible numbers? Why not round to the nearest thousand and use 1,000 and 20 as compatible numbers?

2 How can you find the quotient 500 ÷ 20? What estimate does this give for the number of robots in each box?

3 Look at the second **Model It**. Why do you multiply 21 by multiples of 10? Could you multiply 21 by multiples of 5 instead of by multiples of 10?

4 Look at the table. Between which two numbers is a good estimate for the number of robots packed in each box? Explain how you know.

5 What do the methods of estimating quotients in the **Model Its** have in common?

6 REFLECT

Look back at your **Try It**, strategies by classmates, and **Model Its**. Which models or strategies do you like best for estimating quotients? Explain.

....

....

....

APPLY IT

Use what you just learned to solve these problems.

7 Estimate the quotient 342 ÷ 38. Show your work.

Solution ....

8 Estimate the quotient 1,103 ÷ 23. Show your work.

Solution ....

9 Camille arranged 238 chairs into equal rows of 14 chairs. Which of the following is the best estimate for the number of rows she made?

Ⓐ a number close to 30

Ⓑ about 20

Ⓒ a number between 30 and 40

Ⓓ about 10

©Curriculum Associates, LLC   Copying is not permitted

Practice Estimating Quotients

Study the Example showing how to estimate a quotient with a two-digit divisor. Then solve problems 1–4.

EXAMPLE

Estimate the quotient 1,474 ÷ 22.

Choose compatible numbers that are close to the actual dividend and divisor and easy to multiply and divide using a basic fact.

1,400 and 20 are close to 1,474 and 22.

$2 \times 7 = 14$, $2 \times 70 = 140$, and $20 \times 70 = 1,400$.

$20 \times 70 = 1,400$ is the same as $1,400 \div 20 = 70$.

So, 70 is the estimated quotient for 1,474 ÷ 22.

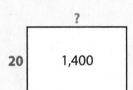

---

1   Look at the Example. You can also multiply 22 by **multiples of 10** to estimate the quotient 1,474 ÷ 22.

a. Complete the table.

Multiple of 10	10	20	30	40	50	60	70	80
22 × Multiple of 10	220	440	660	880	1,100			

b. Complete the statement below with two numbers from the table.

The dividend 1,474 is between .... and ....

c. What is a good estimate for the quotient 1,474 ÷ 22?

2 Which of the following is the best estimate for the quotient 713 ÷ 31?

Ⓐ a number between 10 and 20

Ⓑ a number close to 40

Ⓒ a number close to 35

Ⓓ a number between 20 and 30

3 A beverage company makes 1,008 bottles of water and packs them into boxes. The company packs 24 bottles in each box. Estimate how many boxes of water bottles the company packs. Show your work.

Solution ....

4 Marcus builds 2,744 kites for a 14-day summer kite festival. He plans to give away about the same number of kites each day. He gives away 492 kites the first two days. Did Marcus stick to his plan? Use estimation to explain. Show your work.

Solution ....

   ©Curriculum Associates, LLC   Copying is not permitted

Develop Using Estimation and Area Models to Divide

Read and try to solve the problem below.

> A factory produces 768 buses and puts them in 24 buildings. Each building has the same number of buses. How many buses are in each building? Estimate and then solve.

TRY IT

 **Math Toolkit**
- base-ten blocks
- base-ten grid paper
- grid paper
- index cards

DISCUSS IT

Ask your partner: Do you agree with me? Why or why not?

Tell your partner: I agree with you about . . . because . . .

©Curriculum Associates, LLC   Copying is not permitted

Explore different ways to understand how to divide whole numbers using estimation and area models.

> **A factory produces 768 buses and puts them in 24 buildings. Each building has the same number of buses. How many buses are in each building? Estimate and then solve.**

MODEL IT

You can use the relationship between multiplication and division to estimate the quotient.

$768 \div 24 = ?$ and $24 \times ? = 768$

Multiply 24 by **multiples of 10** to estimate the quotient. You can organize your work in a table.

Number of buses in each building	Total number of buses
10	240
20	480
30	720
40	960

The quotient is between **30** and **40**.

MODEL IT

You can use an area model to solve a division problem with a two-digit divisor.

The area model breaks up the problem $768 \div 24$ into parts.

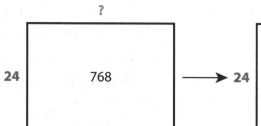

	?
24	768

→

	30	+	2
24	(24 × 30 = 720) 768 − 720 **48**		(24 × 2 = 48) 48 − 48 0

©Curriculum Associates, LLC   Copying is not permitted

CONNECT IT

Now you will use the problem from the previous page to help you understand how to divide whole numbers using estimation and area models.

1 In the first **Model It**, how do you know the quotient is between 30 and 40?

2 Look at the second **Model It**. The number 24 is multiplied by which estimate, 30 or 40, to start the area model work? Why do you think the other number was not used?

3 What does the expression 30 + 2 above the area model represent?

4 Explain why the numbers 30 and 2 can be called *partial quotients*.

5 Explain how an area model can help you break apart a division problem to make it easier to solve.

6 REFLECT

Look back at your **Try It**, strategies by classmates, and **Model Its**. Which models or strategies do you like best for dividing whole numbers? Explain.

....

....

....

APPLY IT

Use what you just learned to solve these problems.

7 In the problem on the previous page, 768 ÷ 24, you first estimated and then used an area model to find the quotient. Describe how can you use multiplication to check that you have the correct quotient.

Show your work for the check.

8 Dante has 468 cards in his sports card collection. He buys cards in packages of 12. Complete the table and give an estimate for how many packages of cards Dante has bought.

Number of packages	10	20	30	40	50
Number of sports cards					

Solution ....

9 Refer to the situation in problem 8. Complete the area model to find the quotient 468 ÷ 12. How many packages of sports cards did Dante buy?

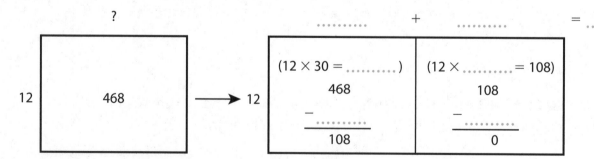

Solution ....

©Curriculum Associates, LLC   Copying is not permitted

Practice Using Estimation and Area Models to Divide

Study the Example showing how to estimate and use area
models to divide. Then solve problems 1–4.

EXAMPLE

A donut shop sells donuts in boxes that each contain 13 donuts.
If 728 donuts were sold in one day, how many boxes of donuts were sold?

Multiply 13 by multiples of 10 to help you estimate the quotient. Make a table.

Number of boxes	10	20	30	40	50	60
Number of donuts	130	260	390	520	650	780

Because 728 is between 650 and 780, the quotient is between 50 and 60.

Use 50 as the first partial quotient in an area model for 728 ÷ 13.

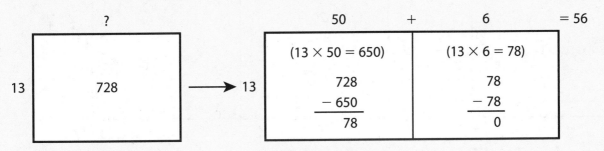

728 ÷ 13 = 56. The donut shop sold 56 boxes of donuts.

---

1 The area model in the Example shows how to break apart the problem 728 ÷ 13
into parts.

a. What was 13 multiplied by first? ....

b. What equation in the area model shows this? ....

c. Why do you subtract 650 from 728?

d. What is the second partial quotient? ....

©Curriculum Associates, LLC   Copying is not permitted

2   The table can be used to estimate the quotient 851 ÷ 37. Which of the following is the best estimate of the quotient?

Multiple of 10	10	20	30	40
37 × Multiple of 10	370	740	1,110	1,480

Ⓐ a number between 30 and 40

Ⓑ about 15

Ⓒ a number between 20 and 30

Ⓓ about 42

3   Complete the steps for using an area model to find the quotient 851 ÷ 37.

851 ÷ 37 is the same as .... × ? = ...

851 ÷ 37 = ...

4   Which of the following equations cannot be used to represent the area model?

Ⓐ 42 × ? = 4,326

Ⓑ 42 + 4,326 = ?

Ⓒ 4,326 ÷ ? = 42

Ⓓ 4,326 ÷ 42 = ?

   ©Curriculum Associates, LLC   Copying is not permitted

Develop Using Area Models and Partial Quotients to Divide

Read and try to solve the problem below.

> A grocery store only sells eggs by the dozen. There are 12 eggs in 1 dozen. If there are 1,248 eggs in stock, how many dozens of eggs are there?

TRY IT

🧰 **Math Toolkit**
- base-ten blocks
- base-ten grid paper
- grid paper
- index cards

DISCUSS IT

Ask your partner: Why did you choose that strategy?

Tell your partner: I knew . . . so I . . .

©Curriculum Associates, LLC   Copying is not permitted

Explore different ways to record partial products when dividing multi-digit whole numbers.

> A grocery store only sells eggs by the dozen. There are 12 eggs in 1 dozen. If there are 1,248 eggs in stock, how many dozens of eggs are there?

MODEL IT

You can use an area model to record partial quotients.

Estimate to determine the first partial quotient for $1,248 \div 12$.

1,200 and 12 are compatible numbers close to the dividend and divisor.

$12 \times 100 = 1,200$, so you can use 100 as the first partial quotient in an area model.

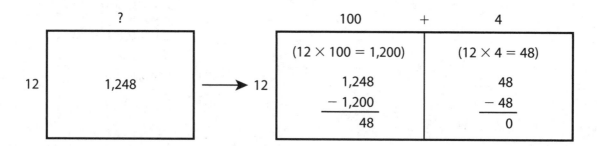

	?
12	1,248

$\longrightarrow$

	100	+	4
12	($12 \times 100 = 1,200$) $\begin{array}{r} 1,248 \\ -1,200 \\ \hline 48 \end{array}$		($12 \times 4 = 48$) $\begin{array}{r} 48 \\ -48 \\ \hline 0 \end{array}$

MODEL IT

You can use a vertical format to record partial quotients.

$$
\begin{array}{r}
4 \quad \longleftarrow \text{second partial quotient} \\
100 \quad \longleftarrow \text{first partial quotient} \\
12\overline{)1,248} \quad \longleftarrow \text{How many groups of 12 in 1,200?} \\
-1,200 \\
\hline
48 \quad \longleftarrow \text{How many groups of 12 in 48?} \\
-48 \\
\hline
0
\end{array}
$$

©Curriculum Associates, LLC Copying is not permitted

CONNECT IT

Now you will use the problem from the previous page to help you understand how to record partial products in a vertical format.

1 Look at the second **Model It**. How many hundreds are in the dividend? ....

How many groups of 12 are in 1,200? ....
Notice that this first partial quotient is written above the bar.

2 After writing the first partial quotient above the bar, you write the number 1,200 under the dividend. What equation in the area model shows where the number

1,200 comes from? ....

3 Why is 1,200 subtracted from 1,248?

4 How does the area model relate to finding the second partial quotient?

5 Explain how to use the partial quotients to find 1,248 ÷ 12. How many dozens of eggs does the grocery store have?

6 Describe how to divide using partial quotients.

7 REFLECT

Look back at your **Try It**, strategies by classmates, and **Model Its**. Which models or strategies do you like best for recording partial products? Explain.

....

....

Lesson 5 Divide Whole Numbers **95**

APPLY IT

Use what you just learned to solve these problems.

8 What is the quotient 583 ÷ 11? Show your work.

Solution ....

9 Carlos has 1,134 pennies. He puts an equal number of pennies into 27 different glass jars. How many pennies are in each jar? Show your work.

Solution ....

10 Which of the following pairs of numbers are partial quotients for 594 ÷ 18?

Ⓐ 50 and 5

Ⓑ 40 and 4

Ⓒ 30 and 3

Ⓓ 20 and 15

©Curriculum Associates, LLC   Copying is not permitted

Practice Using Area Models and Partial Quotients to Divide

Study the Example showing division with a two-digit divisor using partial quotients. Then solve problems 1–5.

EXAMPLE

Find 1,386 ÷ 22.

To divide using partial quotients, estimate a number that can be multiplied by the divisor to get a product less than or equal to the dividend. Then subtract the product from the dividend. Repeat these steps until you reach a number less than the divisor.

$$
\begin{array}{r}
3 \\
60 \\
22\overline{)1,386} \\
-\ 1,320 \\
\hline
66 \\
-\ 66 \\
\hline
0
\end{array}
$$

→ How many groups of 20 in 1,200? **60**
→ 22 × 60
→ How many groups of 22 in 66? **3**
→ 22 × 3

1,386 ÷ 22 = 63

1 Look at the Example. For the first step, Jaime thought: *How many groups of 20 in 1,400? There are 70*. If he continues with the division steps, when will he know that his first estimate of 70 is too high?

2 Multiply 14 by multiples of 10 to complete the table.

Multiple of 10	10	20	30	40	50	60
14 × Multiple of 10	140	280			700	

Write a multiple of 10 from the table to show the greatest partial quotient to start with for each division problem below.

a. 14)462   **b.** 14)350   **c.** 14)798   **d.** 14)588

3 Use an area model to find the quotient 504 ÷ 14.

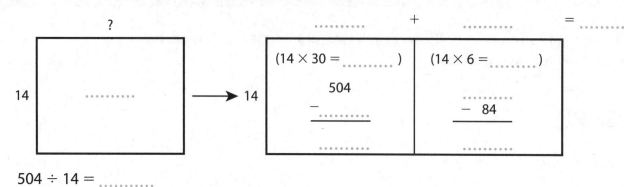

?

14 | ....

14 | (14 × 30 = ...) | (14 × 6 = ...)
504 | ....
− .... | − 84
.... | ....

.... + ... = ...

504 ÷ 14 = ...

4 Find the quotient 504 ÷ 14 using the partial quotient method shown in the Example. Show your work.

Solution ....

DONATION BOX

5 A hunger relief program ships boxes that hold 25 pounds of food. How many boxes will 2,350 pounds of food fill? Show your work.

Solution ....

©Curriculum Associates, LLC Copying is not permitted

Refine Dividing Whole Numbers

Complete the Example below. Then solve problems 1–8.

EXAMPLE

Each package has 21 pieces of chalk. How many packages can be made with 1,701 pieces of chalk?

Look at how you could show your work using partial quotients.

```
        1
       80
   21)1,701
     − 1,680  ← 21 × 80
        21
      − 21  ← 21 × 1
         0
```

Solution ....

> Why is 80 a good number to use as a first partial quotient?

PAIR/SHARE
How can you use multiplication to check that the quotient is correct?

APPLY IT

1 A water cooler holds 1,284 ounces of water. How many more 6-ounce glasses than 12-ounce glasses can be filled from a full cooler? Show your work.

> You can first estimate how many glasses of each size can be filled.

PAIR/SHARE
Explain how you found your estimate.

Solution ....

2 Each student needs 35 craft sticks for an art project. The art teacher has 7,140 craft sticks. How many students can get craft sticks from the teacher? Show your work.

> What numbers can I use to estimate the quotient?

Solution ....

PAIR/SHARE
Explain how to check the answer to a division problem.

3 Harrison creates balloon animals for different events. He has 6,440 balloons. He wants to use the same number of balloons for each of 28 events. How many balloons can Harrison use at each event?

Ⓐ 23

Ⓑ 203

Ⓒ 230

Ⓓ 2,030

Tina chose Ⓐ as the correct answer. How did she get that answer?

> What will be the greatest place in the quotient?

PAIR/SHARE
Does Tina's answer make sense?

©Curriculum Associates, LLC Copying is not permitted

4 Mr. Kovich writes the problem $32 \times \triangle = 1{,}696$ on the board. Write a division equation that can be used to find the value of the triangle. Then find the value of the triangle. Show your work.

Solution ....

5 Vera makes a table to help solve the problem $672 \div 16$.

10	20	30	40	50	60
160	320	480	640	800	960

Choose the correct option to fill in each blank below.

The quotient $672 \div 16$ is between _____

Ⓐ 20   Ⓑ 30   Ⓒ 40   Ⓓ 60

and _____.

Ⓐ 30   Ⓑ 40   Ⓒ 50   Ⓓ 60

6 Lisa's camera has 2,048 megabytes of memory for storing pictures. She has already used half this amount. A high-quality picture uses 16 megabytes of memory. How many high-quality pictures can Lisa store with the remaining memory?

Lesson 5 Divide Whole Numbers   **101**

7 Mr. Sullivan is organizing teams for the middle school's annual field day. There are 8 classes at the school and 21 students in each class.

Part A What is the total number of students at the school?

.... students

Part B Mr. Sullivan wants to have 12 students on each team. How many teams will there be?

.... teams

Part C How many fewer students will be on each team if he decides to have 24 teams? Explain your answer using diagrams, pictures, mathematical expressions, and/or words.

.... fewer students

8 MATH JOURNAL

Explain what you would do first to divide 1,260 by 28. Tell why it would be your first step.

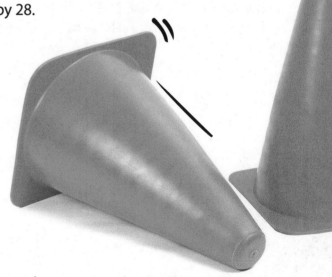

☑ SELF CHECK Go back to the Unit 1 Opener and see what you can check off.

©Curriculum Associates, LLC Copying is not permitted

In this unit you learned to . . .

Skill	Lesson
Find the volume of a solid figure by counting unit cubes.	1, 2
Find volume by using a formula.	3
Break apart a solid figure into rectangular prisms to find its volume.	3
Multiply multi-digit whole numbers, for example: $410 \times 16 = 6,560$.	4
Divide a multi-digit whole number by a two-digit number, for example: $2,812 \div 38 = 74$.	5

Think about what you have learned.

Use words, numbers, and drawings.

1 Two important things I learned are . . .

2 I would like to learn more about how to . . .

3 I still need to work on . . .

Solve Multiplication and Division Problems

Study an Example Problem and Solution

SMP 1 Make sense of problems and persevere in solving them.

Read this problem about multiplying multi-digit numbers. Then look at Beau's solution to this problem.

Worm Farm

Beau likes to recycle. He is going to have a fair to show recycling ideas. One of his ideas is to start a worm farm where he can recycle kitchen scraps from people in his school. He gathers this information.

RED WORM PRICES

1,050 worms $25
2,950 worms $72

My Data

- 2,000 worms can eat about 1 pound of food in 1 day.
- I can collect 195 to 215 pounds of scraps each week.

Show how to find the number of worms Beau needs for this amount of scraps.

- Tell how many and what size packages Beau can buy to get this many worms.

- Give the total cost of buying the worms.

Read the sample solution on the next page. Then look at the checklist below. Find and mark parts of the solution that match the checklist.

✓ PROBLEM-SOLVING CHECKLIST

☐ Tell what is known.

☐ Tell what the problem is asking.

☐ Show all your work.

☐ Show that the solution works.

a. **Circle** something that is known.

b. **Underline** something that you need to find.

c. **Draw a box around** what you do to solve the problem.

d. **Put a checkmark** next to the part that shows the solution works.

©Curriculum Associates, LLC   Copying is not permitted

BEAU'S SOLUTION

- **I already know** that the amount of kitchen scraps is between 195 to 215 pounds. I'll use 200 pounds to make an estimate.

- **I need to find** about how many worms are needed to recycle 200 pounds of scraps each week.

- **I also know** that 2,000 worms eat 1 pound of scraps in 1 day. That means 2,000 worms eat 7 pounds of scraps in 7 days, or 1 week.

- **I can estimate** that 200 is about 30 times 7. So, I need about 30 times 2,000 worms for 200 pounds of scraps.
  $$2,000 \times 30 = 60,000$$
  I need about 60,000 worms.

- **Now I can look for ways to get about 60,000 worms.**
  2,950 is about 3,000 and $3,000 \times 20 = 60,000$.

- **I'll start with 20 packages of 2,950 worms.**

$$\begin{array}{r} 2,950 \\ \times\ \ 20 \\ \hline 59,000 \end{array}$$

- **Then, I'll subtract to find how many more worms I need.**
  $$60,000 - 59,000 = 1,000$$

  I need 1 package of 1,050 worms to get 1,000 more worms.

  The total number of worms is $59,000 + 1,250$, or 60,250.

  This is close to 60,000.

- **Multiply to find the total cost.**

$$\begin{array}{l} \$25 \times 1\ =\quad\ \ \$25 \\ \$72 \times 20 =\ \underline{+\ \$1,440} \\ \qquad\qquad\qquad\ \$1,465 \end{array}$$

Hi, I'm Beau. Here's how I solved this problem.

Since the amount of kitchen scraps is not exact, I can estimate.

Here I used the exact number of worms in the package.

There may be more than 200 pounds of scraps some months. It's okay to have more worms.

Try Another Approach

There are many ways to solve problems. Think about how you might solve the Worm Farm problem in a different way.

Worm Farm

Beau likes to recycle. He is going to have a fair to show recycling ideas. One of his ideas is to start a worm farm where he can recycle kitchen scraps from people in his school. He gathers this information.

RED WORM PRICES

1,050 worms $25
2,950 worms $72

My Data

- 2,000 worms can eat about 1 pound of food in 1 day.

- I can collect 195 to 215 pounds of scraps each week.

Show how to find the number of worms Beau needs for this amount of scraps.

- Tell how many and what size packages Beau can buy to get this many worms.

- Give the total cost of buying the worms.

PLAN IT

Answer these questions to help you start thinking about a plan.

A. Will you use a lesser or greater amount of kitchen scraps to estimate the number of worms? Explain why.

b. How could you solve the problem by finding the amount of kitchen scraps there will be in 1 day?

   ©Curriculum Associates, LLC   Copying is not permitted

SOLVE IT

Find a different solution for the Worm Farm problem. Show all your work on a separate sheet of paper.

You may want to use the Problem-Solving Tips to get started.

PROBLEM-SOLVING TIPS

- **Models** You might want to use . . .
  - partial products.
  - area models.

- **Word Bank**

estimate	total	about
multiply	subtract	close to

- **Sentence Starters**

- To make an estimate, I can use _____

- There are _____ worms in _____

☑ **PROBLEM-SOLVING CHECKLIST**

Make sure that you . . .
- ☐ tell what you know.
- ☐ tell what you need to do.
- ☐ show all your work.
- ☐ show that the solution works.

REFLECT

Use Mathematical Practices As you work through the problem, discuss these questions with a partner.

- **Be Precise** Why is it appropriate to use an estimate with this problem?

- **Make an Argument** Why did you choose the numbers you did for your estimates?

Discuss Models and Strategies

Read the problem. Write a solution on a separate sheet of paper. Remember, there can be lots of ways to solve a problem!

Goldfish Pool

Sweet T is helping design a small goldfish pool to be built for the fair.

The pool will be shaped like the diagram shown. The two ends are the same depth. The middle section is deeper.

Pool Plans

- The total length is between 10 and 16 feet.
- The width is between 6 and 8 feet.
- The deepest part of the pool is no more than 4 feet deep.
- The total volume is 300 cubic feet or less.

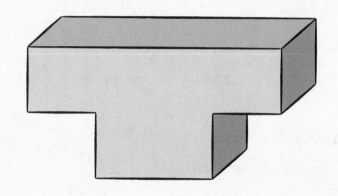

What should the dimensions of the pool be? What will the volume of the pool be?

©Curriculum Associates, LLC   Copying is not permitted

PLAN IT AND SOLVE IT

Find a solution to the Goldfish Pool problem.

- Find the dimensions of the pool.

- Verify that the lengths, widths, and depths you chose meet all of the requirements in the pool plans.

- Find the volume of the pool.

PROBLEM-SOLVING TIPS

- **Questions**
  - How deep will the shallow section be? The deep section?
  - How can you divide the solid figure into rectangular prisms?

- **Word Bank**

rectangular prism	length	volume
solid figure	width	cubic feet

☑ **PROBLEM-SOLVING CHECKLIST**

Make sure that you . . .
- ☐ tell what you know.
- ☐ tell what you need to do.
- ☐ show all your work.
- ☐ show that the solution works.

REFLECT

Use Mathematical Practices As you work through the problem, discuss these questions with a partner.

- **Use a Model** How can the model help you find appropriate dimensions?

- **Be Precise** What measurement units will you use when you work out the solution? Explain.

Persevere On Your Own

Read the problems. Write a solution on a separate sheet of paper.

Robot Area

Beau plans to bring his recycled robots to the fair. Guests can buy tickets to play with the robots. Beau needs to rope off an area of the fairgrounds to keep his robots in sight. Read his notes.

Robot Area Notes

- The area should be rectangular.
- It needs to be more than 100 feet long and less than 100 feet wide.
- The area needs to be between 7,500 and 10,000 square feet.

What dimensions should the robot area have?

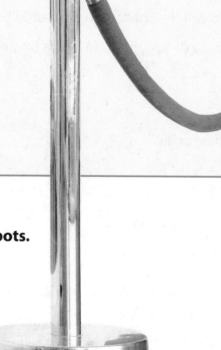

SOLVE IT

Describe an area that Beau can rope off for his robots.

- Give the length and width of the area.
- Give the area in square feet.
- Explain why your measurements work.

REFLECT

Use Mathematical Practices After you complete the task, choose one of these questions to discuss with a partner.

- **Use Structure** How did you use place-value ideas to think about numbers that would work?

- **Persevere** Did you try different combinations of numbers before deciding on a final answer? Explain.

©Curriculum Associates, LLC   Copying is not permitted

Layered Dessert

Sweet T is making his favorite layered dessert to bring to the fair.
Read his notes.

Layered Dessert Notes

- Cut brownies, marshmallows, and cake into cubes.
- First layer is brownie cubes.
- Second layer is marshmallow cubes.
- Third layer is cake cubes.
- Use more than 3 layers.
- You choose the thickness of each layer.
- Repeat layers as many times as you want to fill the bowl.

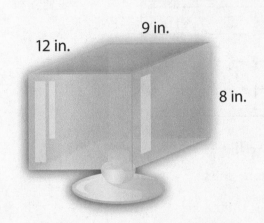

The picture above shows the container Sweet T uses to make the dessert.
How many layers should Sweet T use? How thick should each layer be?

SOLVE IT

Help Sweet T make a plan.

- Tell which item is in each layer.
- Give the length, width, and volume of each layer.
- Find the total volume of the completed dessert.

REFLECT

Use Mathematical Practices After you complete the task, choose one
of these questions to discuss with a partner.

- **Use a Model** What models did you use and how did they help you find a solution?

- **Persevere** What did you do to get through any difficult parts of the solution?

Unit 1 Math in Action Solve Multiplication and Division Problems

1 Which unit of measure can be used to express the volume of the prism?

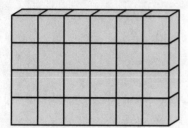

Ⓐ unit squares

Ⓑ square units

Ⓒ cubic units

Ⓓ units

2 Kyle has an aquarium in the shape of a rectangular prism. The aquarium is 24 inches long and has a height of 10 inches. The volume of the aquarium is 2,880 cubic inches. What is the width, in inches, of the aquarium?

3 The solid figure below is made up of two rectangular prisms.

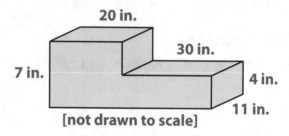

20 in.

30 in.

7 in.

4 in.

11 in.

[not drawn to scale]

What is the volume of the solid figure?

Ⓐ 5,170 cubic inches

Ⓑ 2,970 cubic inches

Ⓒ 2,860 cubic inches

Ⓓ 1,980 cubic inches

4 Which equations are true?

Ⓐ $61 \times 5 = 3,050 \div 10$

Ⓑ $381 \times 27 = 1,143 \div 9$

Ⓒ $854 \times 63 = 53,802$

Ⓓ $562 \times 42 = 23,604$

Ⓔ $72 \times 30 = 270$

©Curriculum Associates, LLC   Copying is not permitted

5 A theater has 3,150 seats. All of the seats are arranged in 42 equal rows. How many seats are in each row? Show your work.

Solution ....

6 Tell if the expression can be used to find the volume, in cubic centimeters, of the rectangular prism below.

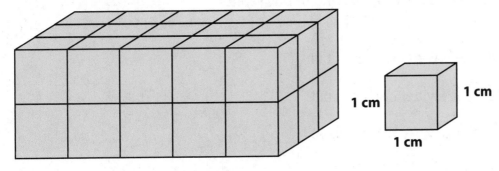

1 cm   1 cm   1 cm

	Yes	**No**
15×2	Ⓐ	Ⓑ
$(5 + 3) \times 2$	Ⓒ	Ⓓ
$15 + 15$	Ⓔ	Ⓕ
$5 + 3 + 2$	Ⓖ	Ⓗ
$15 + 2$	Ⓘ	Ⓙ

Performance Task

Answer the questions and show all your work on separate paper.

Jack wants to make a terrarium for the science fair. The first steps of the instructions are shown below.

Checklist

Did you . . .
- ☐ draw a diagram?
- ☐ use a formula?

How to make a terrarium:

Step 1 Fill the bottom of the tank with a 2-inch layer of small rocks.

Step 2 Add a layer of soil. There should be 5 inches from the top of the soil to the top of the tank.

Jack already has one cubic foot (1,728 cubic inches) of soil and 576 cubic inches of small rocks to use. Now he has to choose a tank. Which of the tanks below can he use without having to buy more rocks and soil?

Tank A: 18 inches long, 15 inches wide, 15 inches tall

Tank B: 24 inches long, 12 inches wide, 12 inches tall

Tank C: 21 inches long, 18 inches wide, 10 inches tall

REFLECT

Use Mathematical Practices After you complete the task, choose one of the following questions to answer.

- **Use Reasoning** Why is the height of the soil layer different for each tank?

- **Model** How does drawing and labeling a diagram help you solve the problem?

Draw or write to show examples for each term.

algorithm a set of routine steps used to solve problems.

My Example

base (of a prism) one side of a prism, usually considered to be the side shown as the bottom of the prism. In the volume formula $V = B \times h$, B represents the area of the base of the prism.

My Example

cubic unit the volume of a unit cube.

My Example

distributive property when one of the factors of a product is written as a sum, multiplying each addend by the other factor before adding does not change the product. For example, $3 \times 12 = (3 \times 10) + (3 \times 2)$.

My Example

face a flat surface of a solid shape.

My Example

inverse operations operations that undo each other. For example, addition and subtraction are inverse operations, and multiplication and division are inverse operations.

My Example

©Curriculum Associates, LLC   Copying is not permitted.

plane figure a two-dimensional figure, such as a circle, triangle, or rectangle.

My Example

rectangular prism a solid figure with six rectangular faces.

My Example

solid figure a three-dimensional figure.

My Example

unit cube a cube with side lengths of 1 unit. A unit cube is said to have one cubic unit of volume, and can be used to measure the volume of a solid figure.

My Example

unit square a square with side lengths of 1 unit. A unit square is said to have one square unit of area, and can be used to measure the area of a plane figure.

My Example

volume the amount of space inside a solid figure. Volume is measured in cubic units such as cubic inches.

My Example

©Curriculum Associates, LLC Copying is not permitted.

☑ SELF CHECK

Before starting this unit, check off the skills you know below. As you complete each lesson, see how many more skills you can check off!

I can . . .	Before	After
Recognize that a digit in one place represents 10 times as much as it represents in the place to its right and $\frac{1}{10}$ of what it represents in the place to its left.	☐	☐
Use patterns to understand multiplying and dividing whole numbers and decimals by powers of 10.	☐	☐
Read and write decimals in different forms, for example: $80.63 = 8 \times 10 + 6 \times \frac{1}{10} + 3 \times \frac{1}{100}$.	☐	☐
Compare decimals, for example: 3.47 > 3.096.	☐	☐
Round decimals, for example: 6.274 rounded to the nearest tenth is 6.3.	☐	☐
Add and subtract decimals, for example: 20.08 + 5.15 = 25.23.	☐	☐
Add and subtract fractions with unlike denominators.	☐	☐
Estimate sums and differences of fractions or decimals.	☐	☐

©Curriculum Associates, LLC   Copying is not permitted

Build Your Vocabulary

Math Vocabulary

Complete the blank boxes with the corresponding vocabulary terms.

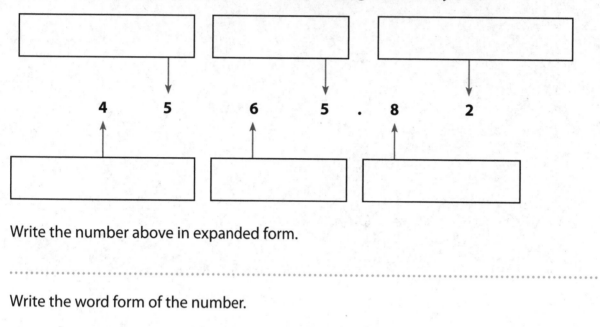

Write the number above in expanded form.

....

Write the word form of the number.

....

Academic Vocabulary

Place a check next to the academic words you know. Then use the words to complete the sentences.

☐ analyze   ☐ defend   ☐ format   ☐ relationship

1 You can .... a problem by examining its parts carefully.

2 Sometimes you have to .... your answer to show why it is correct.

3 In STEM classes, you can examine the .... between science, technology, engineering, and math.

4 It's important to use the correct .... when setting up a division problem.

©Curriculum Associates, LLC   Copying is not permitted

Dear Family,

This week your child is exploring place value in whole numbers and decimal numbers.

We use a number system called **base ten**. It is based on a pattern of tens. The models below show the pattern of tens in whole numbers and decimals. Each place value is 10 times the place value to its right.

Thousands	Hundreds	Tens	Ones
1 thousand is **10 times** 1 hundred	1 hundred is **10 times** 1 ten	1 ten is **10 times** 1 one	1 one
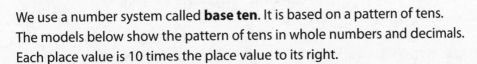			
1,000	100	10	1

Ones	Tenths	Hundredths
1 whole is **10 times** 1 tenth	1 tenth is **10 times** 1 hundredth	1 hundredth
1	0.1	0.01

Understanding place value helps your child think about and use different ways to add, subtract, multiply, and divide numbers.

Invite your child to share what he or she knows about place value by doing the following activity together.

ACTIVITY DECIMAL PLACE VALUE

Do this activity with your child to explore decimal place-value relationships.

Work together with your child to shade models to understand decimal place value.

- Have your child shade in the decimal grids below to represent the number that is shown below each grid.

- Ask your child to explain how each pair of grids shows that the number on the right is 10 times the number on the left grid.

Each grid represents 1 whole.

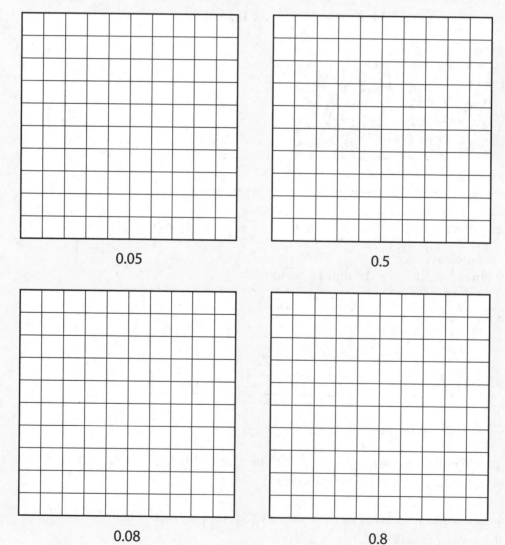

0.05

0.5

0.08

0.8

©Curriculum Associates, LLC   Copying is not permitted

Explore **Place Value**

How is place value related
to the number 10?

Florida Standards

5.NBT.1.1 Recognize that in a multi-digit number, a digit in one place represents 10 times as much as it represents in the place to its right and $\frac{1}{10}$ of what it represents in the place to its left.

MODEL IT
Complete the problems below.

1 Look at the place-value models for whole numbers. Write the missing factor in each equation to show how ones, tens, hundreds, and thousands are related.

Thousands	Hundreds	Tens	Ones
$1{,}000 = \underline{\quad} \times 100$	$100 = \underline{\quad} \times 10$	$10 = \underline{\quad} \times 1$	1

2 Write the missing numbers in the equations below these place-value models for **decimals** to show how hundredths, tenths, and ones are related.

Ones	Tenths	Hundredths
$1.0 = \underline{\quad} \times 0.1$	$0.1 = \underline{\quad} \times 0.01$	0.01

3 Look at your equations in problems 1 and 2. Explain how the value of each place compares to the value of the place to its right.

DISCUSS IT

• How are relationships between decimal place values like relationships between whole number place values?

• I think we call our number system **base ten** because . . .

MODEL IT

Complete the problems below.

4 Fill in the blanks in the diagram to show how the values of the numbers change from row to row in the table. Extend the pattern to fill in the top and bottom rows.

5 What happens to the position and value of the digit **1** when you multiply by 10?

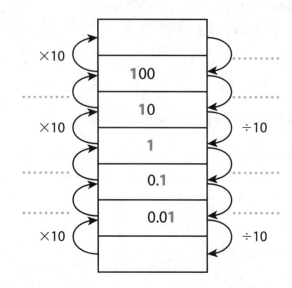

6 What happens to the position and value of the digit **1** when you divide by 10?

7 What do you think is the value of the digit 1 in the number you wrote in the last row of the table? Explain.

8 Dividing a number by 10 is the same as finding $\frac{1}{10}$ of the number. Use the phrase "$\frac{1}{10}$ of" or the phrase "10 times" to complete each statement about 1 **thousandth**.

0.001 is .... 0.01. $\frac{1}{100}$ is .... $\frac{1}{1,000}$.

9 **REFLECT**

In which number does the digit 5 have a greater value, 0.05 or 0.005? How many times as great is the value? Explain how you know.

> ## DISCUSS IT
>
> • How are your descriptions of the patterns in the position and value of the digit **1** similar to your partner's? How are they different?
>
> • I think you would show 0.001 on a decimal grid by shading $\frac{1}{10}$ of one small square because . . .

Prepare for Place Value

1   Think about what you know about place value. Fill in each box.
Use words, numbers, and pictures. Show as many ideas as you can.

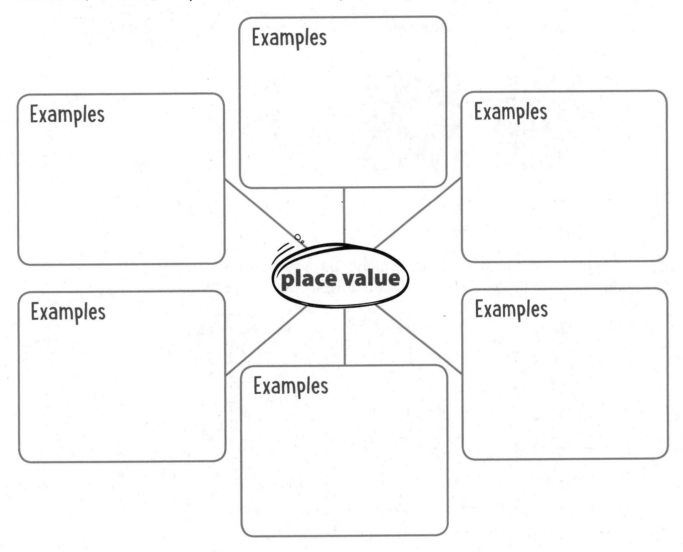

2   Complete each statement with the phrase "$\frac{1}{10}$ of" or the
phrase "10 times."

$\frac{1}{10}$ is .... $\frac{1}{100}$.   0.01 is .... 0.1.

Solve.

3 Write the missing number in each sentence below the base-ten models to show how ones, tens, hundreds, and thousands are related.

Thousands	Hundreds	Tens	Ones
1,000	100 is $\frac{1}{10}$ of	10 is $\frac{1}{10}$ of	1 is $\frac{1}{10}$ of ....

4 Write the missing number in each sentence below the decimal grid models to show how hundredths, tenths, and ones are related.

Ones	Tenths	Hundredths
1.0	0.1 is $\frac{1}{10}$ of	0.01 is $\frac{1}{10}$ of ....

5 Look at your sentences in problems 3 and 4. Explain how the value of each place compares to the value of the place to its left.

©Curriculum Associates, LLC   Copying is not permitted

Develop Understanding of Place Value

MODEL IT: DECIMAL GRIDS

Try these three problems.

1 Each decimal grid in models *A*, *B*, and *C* represents 1 whole. Shade each model to show the decimal number below the model.

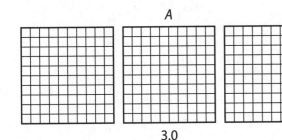

A

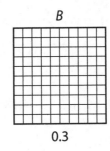

B

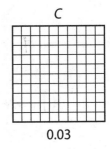

C

3.0   0.3   0.03

2 Complete four different equations that show relationships between the numbers shown in models *A*, *B*, and *C* above.

.... × 10 = ...

.... × 10 = ...

.... ÷ 10 = ...

.... ÷ 10 = ...

3 Finding $\frac{1}{10}$ of a number is the same as multiplying the number by 0.1. Complete each sentence and then write the sentence as a multiplication equation.

a. 0.03 is $\frac{1}{10}$ of ....

    Equation ....

b. .... is $\frac{1}{10}$ of 3.0.

    Equation ....

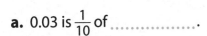

DISCUSS IT

• How did you and your partner figure out what numbers to use in the equations?

• I think the value of the 3 in 0.3 is greater than the value of the 3 in 0.03 because . . .

MODEL IT: NUMBER LINES

Use a number line to show how decimal place values are related.

4 **a.** Fill in the missing labels for the red tick marks on the number lines below.

b. Place a point for the whole number 1 on the first number line, the decimal 0.1 on the second number line, and the decimal 0.01 on the last number line.

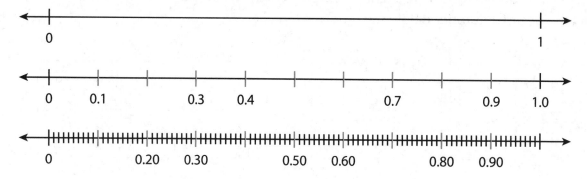

5 How does the distance from 0 to 1 compare to the distance from 0 to 0.1? to the distance from 0 to 0.01?

> **DISCUSS IT**
>
> • How did you and your partner decide where 0.01 is on the last number line?
>
> • I think you can use a number line to show any decimal value because . . .

CONNECT IT

Complete the problems below.

6 How do decimal grids and number lines help you understand the relationship between adjacent place values in our number system?

7 How many times as great is the value of 1.5 than the value of 0.15? Explain.

©Curriculum Associates, LLC   Copying is not permitted

Practice with Place Value

Study how the Example shows place-value patterns. Then solve problems 1–8.

EXAMPLE

Show how the numbers 1, 0.1, and 0.01 are related.

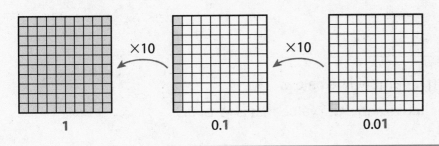

1   0.1   0.01

1 Use the ×10 pattern from the Example to complete each equation.

$$1 = \text{...............} \times 10$$

$$0.1 = \text{...............} \times 10$$

2 The pattern can also be described using division. Use the decimal grids in the Example to complete the equations.

$$1.0 \div 10 = \text{................}$$

$$0.1 \div 10 = \text{................}$$

3 Use the ÷10 pattern to fill in the blanks.

400   ....   0.4   ....

÷ 10

4 How are the decimals 0.009 and 0.09 related? Explain.

©Curriculum Associates, LLC   Copying is not permitted

5 Is the expression equivalent to 0.07?

	Yes	No
0.007 × 10	Ⓐ	Ⓑ
0.7 ÷ 10	Ⓒ	Ⓓ
0.07 × 10	Ⓔ	Ⓕ
0.007 ÷ 10	Ⓖ	Ⓗ

6 **a.** Label the red tick marks on the number line below.

   b. Place a point on the number line to show the value that is $\frac{1}{10}$ of 0.5.

   0   1.00

   c. $\frac{1}{10}$ of 0.5 is ....

   d. Write the sentence in part c as a multiplication equation.

7 Ethan says that the value of 40.7 is 10 times the value of 4.07. Is he correct? Explain.

8 Mya says the value of the 6 in 0.006 is $\frac{1}{10}$ of the value of the 6 in 0.6. Is she correct? Explain.

©Curriculum Associates, LLC Copying is not permitted

Refine Ideas About Place Value

APPLY IT

Complete these problems on your own.

1 CREATE

Shade the models at the right to show how the value of 0.04 is related to the value of 0.4. Then write a division equation to represent the relationship.

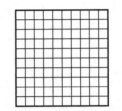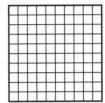

Equation ....

2 ANALYZE

Kiran showed 0.08 with the model below.

What is wrong with Kiran's model? Describe how the length she shaded relates to the length that she should have shaded. How can Kiran change her model to show 0.08?

3 COMPARE

How does the value of the digit 8 in 1.8 compare to the value of the digit 8 in 486? Explain.

PAIR/SHARE
Discuss your solutions for these three problems with a partner.

©Curriculum Associates, LLC   Copying is not permitted

Use what you have learned to complete problem 4.

4 A small beetle has a mass of 0.002 kilogram. A bee has a mass of 0.02 kilogram. A small brick has a mass of 0.2 kilogram.

Part A Write each measurement in the place-value chart below.

Object	Tens	Ones	.	Tenths	Hundredths	Thousandths
beetle						
bee						
brick						

Part B Shade the models to compare the mass of the bee to the mass of the brick. Then write a sentence to describe the relationship between the two masses.

Bee

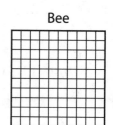

Brick

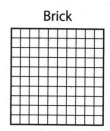

Part C Explain how many small beetles it would take to equal the mass of 1 small brick. Then write an equation using the measurements to show your answer.

5 MATH JOURNAL

What is the number that has a value 10 times the value of 0.009? Explain.

©Curriculum Associates, LLC   Copying is not permitted

Understand Powers of 10

Dear Family,

This week your child is exploring powers of 10.

Your child is learning that numbers such as 10, 100, or 1,000 can be written as products of the number 10.

These numbers are called **powers of 10**. The **exponent** tells how many times to use 10 as a factor.

$$10 = \mathbf{10} = 10^1$$
$$100 = \mathbf{10 \times 10} = 10^2$$
$$1,000 = \mathbf{10 \times 10 \times 10} = 10^3$$

When you multiply a decimal by a power of 10, the decimal point moves right.

Multiply by 10.

$$0.03 \times 10 = 0.3$$

Move the decimal point one place to the right. The digit in the hundredths place is now in the tenths place.

Multiply by 100 (10 × 10).

$$0.005 \times 100 = 0.5$$

Move the decimal point two places to the right. The digit in the thousandths place is now in the tenths place.

When you divide a decimal by a power of 10, the decimal point moves left.

Divide by 10.

$$0.3 \div 10 = 0.03$$

Move the decimal point one place to the left. The digit in the tenths place is now in the hundredths place.

Divide by 100 (10 × 10).

$$0.5 \div 100 = 0.005$$

Move the decimal point two places to the left. The digit in the tenths place is now in the thousandths place.

Invite your child to share what he or she knows about powers of 10 by doing the following activity together.

ACTIVITY MULTIPLY AND DIVIDE BY POWERS OF 10

Do this activity with your child to explore multiplying and dividing by a power of 10.

Work together with your child to show how the decimal point moves when you multiply or divide a decimal number by a power of 10.

- Have your child write the number 12345 with large digits on a separate sheet of paper or use the number below.

- Have your child place his or her finger between the 3 and 4. Your child's finger represents the decimal point.

- Ask your child to multiply the number by 100 and show the answer by moving the decimal point. (Your child should move his or her finger two places to the right.)

- Ask your child to divide the number from the previous step by 10 and show the answer by moving the decimal point. (Your child should move his or her finger one place to the left.)

- Ask your child to show you another multiplication or division by a power of 10. Have your child explain how he or she knows where to move the decimal point.

©Curriculum Associates, LLC   Copying is not permitted

Explore Powers of 10

What patterns can you find when you multiply or divide by 10, 100, or 1,000?

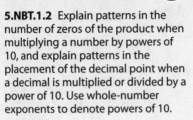

Florida Standards

5.NBT.1.2 Explain patterns in the number of zeros of the product when multiplying a number by powers of 10, and explain patterns in the placement of the decimal point when a decimal is multiplied or divided by a power of 10. Use whole-number exponents to denote powers of 10.

5.NBT.1.1

MODEL IT

Complete the problems below.

1 Numbers like 10, 100, or 1,000 that can be written as a product of tens are called **powers of 10**. Complete the equations to multiply 3 by a power of 10.

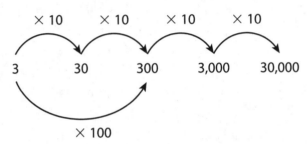

a. $3 \times 10 \times 10 = 3 \times$ ....

$=$ ....

b. $3 \times 10 \times 10 \times 10 = 3 \times$ ....

$=$ ....

c. $3 \times 10 \times 10 \times 10 \times 10 = 3 \times$ ....

$=$ ....

2 Complete the equations to divide 30,000 by a power of 10.

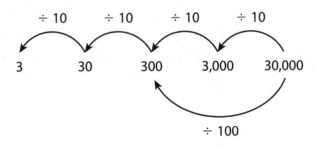

$30,000 \div 100 =$ ....

$30,000 \div 10,000 =$ ....

DISCUSS IT

- How did you and your partner determine the product or quotient in the equations?

- Patterns help me understand how to multiply or divide by numbers like 10, 100, or 1,000 because . . .

MODEL IT

Complete the problems below.

3 You can write a power of 10 using an **exponent**.

The exponent **4** means to use the **base 10** as a factor 4 times.

$$10^4 = 10 \times 10 \times 10 \times 10$$

Complete the table to show different ways to write the first three powers of 10.

Standard Form	Product of Tens	Exponent Form
10	10	10^1
100		10^2
	$10 \times 10 \times 10$	

DISCUSS IT

• What patterns do you notice in multiplying by powers of 10?

• Using exponent form helps me understand place-value relationships because . . .

4 Complete the table to show different ways to write 300, 3,000, and 30,000.

Standard Form	Using a Power of 10	Using Factors of 10	Exponent Form
300	3×100	$3 \times 10 \times 10$	3×10^2
3,000	$3 \times 1,000$	$3 \times$	$3 \times$
30,000	$3 \times$	$3 \times 10 \times 10 \times 10 \times 10$	$3 \times$

5 REFLECT

How do you know how many zeros are in the product 5×10^4? What is the product?

....

....

....

©Curriculum Associates, LLC Copying is not permitted

Prepare for Powers of 10

1 Think about what you know about powers of 10. Fill in each box.
Use words, numbers, and pictures. Show as many ideas as you can.

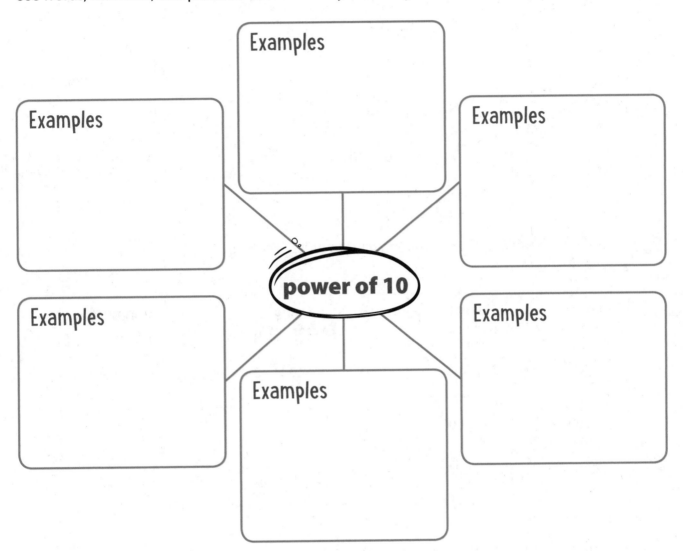

Examples	Examples	Examples
Examples	**power of 10**	Examples
Examples	Examples	

2 Use the diagram to help you find each product.

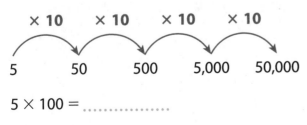

$\times$ **10** $\times$ **10** $\times$ **10** $\times$ **10**

5   50   500   5,000   50,000

$5 \times 100 =$ ....

$5 \times 10,000 =$ ....

©Curriculum Associates, LLC Copying is not permitted

Solve.

3 Complete the table showing different ways to write powers of 10.

Standard Form	Product of Tens	Exponent Form
100	10 × 10	10^2
1,000		10^3
10,000	10 × 10 × 10 × 10	
	10 × 10 × 10 × 10 × 10	

4 Complete the table to show different ways to write 500, 5,000, and 50,000.

Standard Form	Using a Power of 10	Using Factors of 10	Exponent Form
500	5 × 100	5 × 10 × 10	5 × 10^2
5,000	5 × 1,000	5	5 ×
50,000	5 ×	5 × 10 × 10 × 10 × 10	5 ×

5 Rewrite each division equation to show the power of 10 in exponent form. Use the first pair of equations as an example.

$5,000 \div 10 = 500$ ⟶ $5,000 \div 10^1 = 500$

$5,000 \div 100 = 50$ ⟶ $5,000 \div \text{..................} = 50$

$5,000 \div 1,000 = 5$ ⟶ $5,000 \div \text{................} = 5$

©Curriculum Associates, LLC   Copying is not permitted

Develop **Understanding of Powers of 10**

MODEL IT: DECIMAL POINT PATTERNS

Try these two problems.

1 The diagrams below show patterns in the placement of the decimal point each time you multiply or divide a decimal by 10.

Complete the missing numbers in each diagram. The decimal point for each missing number is already placed for you.

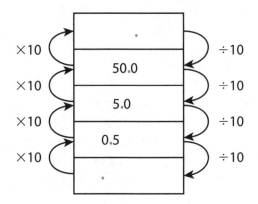

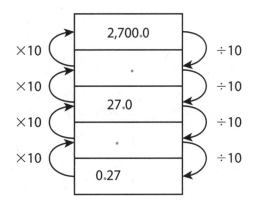

2 Use the decimal point pattern diagrams above to help you find each product or quotient.

$0.5 \times 100 =$ ....

$0.5 \times 10^2 =$ ....

$5 \div 100 =$ ....

$5 \div 10^2 =$ ....

$0.27 \times 1,000 =$ ....

$0.27 \times 10^3 =$ ....

$2,700 \div 1,000 =$ ....

$2,700 \div 10^3 =$ ....

DISCUSS IT

- What happens to the value of a number when you multiply or divide by a power of 10? Why?

- I think multiplying a decimal by 1,000 moves the decimal point three places to the right because . . .

MODEL IT: PLACE-VALUE CHARTS

Use place-value charts to show multiplying and dividing by powers of 10.

3 Complete each row with the product shown to the right of that row.

Ones	.	Tenths	Hundredths	Thousandths
0	.	0	0	4
	.			
	.			
	.			

0.004×10^1

0.004×10^2

0.004×10^3

4 Complete each row with the quotient shown to the right of that row.

Ones	.	Tenths	Hundredths	Thousandths
4	.	0	0	0
	.			
	.			
	.			

$4 \div 10^1$

$4 \div 10^2$

$4 \div 10^3$

DISCUSS IT

- What pattern describes how the decimal point moves when you multiply or divide any decimal by a power of 10?

- I think place-value charts show the pattern of multiplying and dividing by powers of 10 because . . .

CONNECT IT

Complete the problems below.

5 Look at the decimal point pattern diagrams and the place-value charts. Compare how they show patterns in the placement of the decimal point when you multiply (or divide) a decimal by a power of 10.

6 Show how to find the product 0.19×10^3.

©Curriculum Associates, LLC   Copying is not permitted

Practice with Powers of 10

Study how the Example shows multiplying a decimal number by a power of 10. Then solve problems 1–7.

EXAMPLE

Find $10^2 \times 0.004$.

Break 10^2 into the product of tens.

$$10^2 \times 0.004 = 10 \times 10 \times 0.004$$
$$= 10 \times 0.04$$
$$= 0.4$$

The decimal point moves one place to the right for each factor of 10.

$$10^2 \times 0.004 = 0.4$$

1 Write the missing power of 10 in exponential form.

a. $0.04 \times$ .... $= 0.4$ $0.004 \times$ .... $= 4$

b. .... $\times 0.006 = 0.6$ .... $\times 0.006 = 6$

c. $0.007 \times$ .... $= 7$ $0.07 \times$ .... $= 7$

2 Complete the equations to find each product.

a. $8 \times 100 = 8 \times 10^2 =$ ....

b. $8 \times 1,000 = 8 \times$ .... $=$ ....

c. $2 \times$ .... $= 2 \times 10^1 =$ ....

d. $0.02 \times 100 = 0.02 \times$ .... $=$ ....

3 Complete the equations.

a. $0.03 \times 1,000 =$ ....

b. $0.18 \times 100 =$ ....

Vocabulary

power of 10 a number that can be written as a product of tens.

$10 = 10$
$100 = 10 \times 10$
$1,000 = 10 \times 10 \times 10$

exponent the number in a power that tells how many times to use the base as a factor.

10^2 ←exponent
↑
base

$10^2 = 10 \times 10$, or 100

4 Use the place-value chart to show dividing 9 by powers of 10. Complete each row with the quotient shown to the right of the row.

Ones	.	Tenths	Hundredths	Thousandths	
9	.	0	0	0	
	.				$9 \div 10$
	.				$9 \div 10^2$
	.				$9 \div 10^3$

5 Write the quotient.

a. $0.02 \div 10 =$ ....

b. $527 \div 10^2 =$ ....

c. $3 \div 10^3 =$ ....

6 How is the way the decimal point moves when you divide a decimal number by a power of 10 the same as when you multiply by a power of 10? How is it different?

7 Is multiplying by 10^3 the same as multiplying by 10 factors of 3? Explain.

©Curriculum Associates, LLC Copying is not permitted

Refine Ideas About Powers of 10

APPLY IT

Complete these problems on your own.

1 COMPARE

Complete the place-value chart with the products and quotients shown to the right of the chart. Then write a sentence to compare the value of 0.8×10^2 to the value of $0.8 \div 10^2$.

Tens	Ones	.	Tenths	Hundredths	Thousandths	
		.				0.8×10^2
		.				0.8×10^1
	0	.	8	0	0	
		.				$0.8 \div 10^1$
		.				$0.8 \div 10^2$

2 INSPECT

Max says that the product 30×10^4 has exactly four zeros. Is he correct? Explain.

3 EXPLAIN

How do you determine the value of the unknown exponent in the equation $9,700 \div 10^? = 0.97$?

PAIR/SHARE

Discuss your solutions for these three problems with a partner.

Use what you have learned to complete problem 4.

4 Jaime claims that when you multiply a whole number or a decimal by 10^2, the decimal point moves two places to the right.

Salome argues that you move the decimal point two places to the right only when you multiply a decimal by 10^2. Salome says that when you multiply a whole number by 10^2, you can put two extra zeros after the whole number to find the product.

Part A Explain each student's point of view with examples.

Part B Which student is correct? Justify your answer.

5 MATH JOURNAL

Find the value of $80 \div 10^4$. Explain the change in value between 80 and $80 \div 10^4$.

©Curriculum Associates, LLC   Copying is not permitted

Read and Write Decimals

Dear Family,

This week your child is learning how to read and write decimals.

The table below shows different ways to represent the number 5.387.

Standard Form	5.387
Word Form	five and three hundred eighty-seven thousandths
Place-Value Chart	<table><thead><tr><th>Ones</th><th>.</th><th>Tenths</th><th>Hundredths</th><th>Thousandths</th></tr></thead><tbody><tr><td>5</td><td>.</td><td>3</td><td>8</td><td>7</td></tr></tbody></table>
Decimal Expanded Form	$5 + 0.3 + 0.08 + 0.007$ or $5 + 3 \times 0.1 + 8 \times 0.01 + 7 \times 0.001$
Fraction Expanded Form	$5 + \frac{3}{10} + \frac{8}{100} + \frac{7}{1,000}$ or $5 + 3 \times \frac{1}{10} + 8 \times \frac{1}{100} + 7 \times \frac{1}{1,000}$
Mixed Number	$5\frac{387}{1,000}$

Understanding different ways to read and write decimals helps prepare your child for comparing decimals and solving problems with decimals.

Invite your child to share what he or she knows about reading and writing decimals by doing the following activity together.

©Curriculum Associates, LLC   Copying is not permitted

ACTIVITY READING AND WRITING DECIMALS

Do this activity with your child to read and write decimals.

Materials number cube

- Use the two tables below, one for you and one for your child. Have your child roll the number cube. You and your child each write the digit shown on the cube in one place in your place-value chart. You should each write the digit in a different place in your chart.

- Have your child roll the number cube three more times. Write each digit rolled in your place-value charts. For example, if the digits 1, 3, 5, and 6 are rolled, you might write 3.615 and your child might write 5.361.

- Now, write the decimal in word form and in standard form in your charts.

- Ask your child to explain why the order of the digits matters when writing decimals.

Place-Value Chart	Ones	.	Tenths	Hundredths	Thousandths
		.			
Word Form					
Standard Form					

Place-Value Chart	Ones	.	Tenths	Hundredths	Thousandths
		.			
Word Form					
Standard Form					

©Curriculum Associates, LLC Copying is not permitted

Explore Reading and Writing Decimals

In previous lessons, you learned about decimal place value. Use what you know to try to solve the problem below.

> **Jessica reads aloud from a science website.**
> **She comes across the measurement 0.32 meter.**
> **How should she read 0.32 aloud?**
> **Explain how you know.**

Florida Standards

5.NBT.1.3a Read and write decimals to thousandths using base-ten numerals, number names, and expanded form, e.g., 347.392 = $3 \times 100 + 4 \times 10 + 7 \times 1 + 3 \times \left(\frac{1}{10}\right) + 9 \times \left(\frac{1}{100}\right) + 2 \times \left(\frac{1}{1000}\right)$.

TRY IT

 **Math Toolkit**
- base-ten blocks
- base-ten grid paper
- place-value charts
- number lines

DISCUSS IT

Ask your partner: How did you get started?

Tell your partner: I knew . . . so I . . .

CONNECT IT

1 LOOK BACK

Explain how to read 0.32 aloud.

2 LOOK AHEAD

On the previous page, you used words to say the standard form of the decimal 0.32. You can also use **expanded form** to break apart a decimal by place value. You can use either decimals or fractions to write the expanded form of a decimal.

a. Complete each missing number to show two ways to write 0.32 in expanded form using decimals.

0.32 = ... + ...

0.32 = ... × 0.1 + ... × 0.01

b. Complete each missing number to show two ways to write 0.32 in expanded form using fractions.

$0.32 = \dfrac{\square}{10} + \dfrac{\square}{100}$

$0.32 = \text{...............} \times \dfrac{1}{10} + \text{...............} \times \dfrac{1}{100}$

3 REFLECT

How are the different expanded forms of 0.32 alike and different?

....

....

....

....

....

©Curriculum Associates, LLC Copying is not permitted

Develop Reading a Decimal in Word Form

Read and try to solve the problem below.

Josh uses a kitchen scale to weigh some blueberries. The blueberries weigh 0.604 pound. Josh's mom wants to know how much the blueberries weigh. How does Josh say how much the blueberries weigh? Explain your thinking.

TRY IT

Six hundreds o four thousandths

Math Toolkit
- base-ten blocks
- base-ten grid paper
- place-value charts

thousands	hundreds	tens	ones	. and	tenths	hundredths	thousandths
			0	.	6	0	4

where does it end

DISCUSS IT

Ask your partner: Do you agree with me? Why or why not?

Tell your partner: At first, I thought . . .

Explore different ways to understand how to read decimals.

> Josh uses a kitchen scale to weigh some blueberries. The blueberries weigh 0.604 pound. Josh's mom wants to know how much the blueberries weigh. How does Josh say how much the blueberries weigh? Explain your thinking.

[handwritten: Ones Decimal Tenths Tenthredths Hundredths Thousandths | 0 . 6 0 4 | Six and four thousandths]

MODEL IT

You can use place-value understanding to write the expanded form of 0.604. You can then write the number as a fraction.

With decimals:

$$0.604 = 0.6 + 0.004$$

$$0.604 = 6 \times 0.1 + 4 \times 0.001$$

With fractions:

$$0.604 = 6 \times \frac{1}{10} + 4 \times \frac{1}{1,000}$$

$$0.604 = \frac{6}{10} + \frac{4}{1,000}$$

$$0.604 = \frac{600}{1,000} + \frac{4}{1,000}$$

$$0.604 = \frac{604}{1,000}$$

MODEL IT

You can write 0.604 in a place-value chart to show the place value of each digit.

Ones	.	Tenths	Hundredths	Thousandths
0	.	6	0	4

The least place value of 0.604 is thousandths.

[handwritten: Ones Decimal Tenths Hundredths Thousandths | 0 . 6 0 4]

©Curriculum Associates, LLC Copying is not permitted

CONNECT IT
Now you will use the problem from the previous page to help you understand how to read decimals.

1 Look at the place-value chart. What are the names of the four place values in 0.604?

Thousandths

Which of those places has the least value? *Thousandths*

2 Look at the expanded form with fractions. How many thousandths are there altogether in 0.604? *604   604*

3 What is the word form of 0.604?

Six hundred and four thousandths   = 0.604
$= 6.004$

4 What is the word form of 1.604?

One and six hundred four thousandths

5 Explain how reading the digits to the right of the decimal point and knowing the name of the least place value help you read a decimal number. Use the examples 0.604 and 1.604 in your explanation.

Reading the digit to the right of the decimal point and knowing the name of the least place value helps me read a decimal number because when I read the point as an and I'm indicating there's a whole number and little bit more, like 1.604 the whole number is the 1 and 604. Know the place of the least digit help me name correctly the number

6 **REFLECT**

Look back at your **Try It**, strategies by classmates, and **Model Its**. Which models or strategies do you like best for reading a decimal? Explain.

I like more the Model it strategy because it helps keep an order for each of the number and read it easier because I know where is each number.

Ex:

One	.	tenths	hundredths	Thousandths
0	.	6	3	

Sixty three hundredths

Ex: 1.604 One and six 604 thousandths

APPLY IT

Use what you just learned to solve these problems.

7 What is the word form of 0.374? Show your work.

Solution *Three hundred seventy four thousandths.*

8 A number is written in expanded form as
$7 \times 10 + 5 \times \frac{1}{10} + 1 \times \frac{1}{100} + 6 \times \frac{1}{1,000}$.
What is the word form of the number? Show your work.

$$7 \times 10 = 70$$

$$\frac{5}{7} \times \frac{1}{10} = \frac{5}{10} = 5$$

$$\frac{1}{1} \times \frac{1}{100} = \frac{1}{100}$$

$$\frac{6}{1} \times \frac{1}{1,000} = \frac{6}{1000}$$

Seventy and
Five hundred
Sixteen
thousandths

$$= 70 + \frac{5}{10 \times 10} + \frac{1}{100} + \frac{6}{1000} = 70 \frac{516}{1000}$$

Converter to decmm
$70 \quad 516 \div 1000$
$70 = 0,516.$
$= 70,516.$

Solution *Seventy and five hundred sixteen thousandths*

9 What is the word form of 807.057? Show your work.

Solution *Eight - hundred seven and fifty seven thousandths.*

©Curriculum Associates, LLC Copying is not permitted

Read and try to solve the problem below.

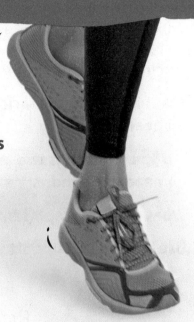

A school holds a running race.

- Abha finishes the race one and sixteen thousandths seconds ahead of Nadia.

- Brianne finishes two and thirty-five hundredths seconds ahead of Chandra.

What decimals represent these measurements?

Use a model to support your answer.

TRY IT

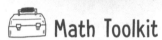 **Math Toolkit**
- base-ten blocks
- base-ten grid paper
- place-value charts

 **DISCUSS IT**

Ask your partner: Why did you choose that strategy?

Tell your partner: The strategy I used to find the answer was . . .

Explore different ways to understand how to write a mixed number given in word form as a decimal in standard form.

> **A school holds a running race.**
>
> • **Abha finishes the race one and sixteen thousandths seconds ahead of Nadia.**
>
> *[handwritten: Decimal point, Tenths, Hundredths, Thousandths 1.0 1 6]*
>
> • **Brianne finishes two and thirty-five hundredths seconds ahead of Chandra.**
>
> *[handwritten: 2 Decimal point Tenths Hundredths Thousands 3 5 10t]*
>
> **What decimals represent these measurements?**
>
> *[handwritten: 1.016 and 2.350]*
>
> **Use a model to support your answer.**

MODEL IT
Model the measurements with mixed numbers and expanded form.

Write mixed numbers to show the number of whole seconds and the fraction of a second given by each measurement. Then expand.

one and sixteen thousandths   *[handwritten: three and nineteen thousands]*   two and thirty-five hundredths

$$1\frac{16}{1,000}$$ *[handwritten: $3\frac{19}{100}$]* $$2\frac{35}{100}$$

$$1+\frac{16}{1,000}$$ $$2+\frac{35}{100}$$

$$1+\frac{10}{1,000}+\frac{6}{1,000}$$ *[handwritten: $3+\frac{19}{100}$]* $$2+\frac{30}{100}+\frac{5}{100}$$

$$1+\frac{1}{100}+\frac{6}{1,000}$$ *[handwritten: $3+\frac{10}{1,000}+\frac{9}{1,000}$]* $$2+\frac{3}{10}+\frac{5}{100}$$

MODEL IT

[handwritten: $3+\frac{1}{100}+\frac{9}{1,000}$]

Use a place-value chart to write the measurements.

Ones	.	Tenths	Hundredths	Thousandths
1	.	0	1	6
2	.	3	5	*[handwritten: 0]*

[handwritten bottom row: 3 . 0 1 9]

16 thousandths is 10 thousandths and 6 thousandths or 1 hundredth and 6 thousandths.

35 hundredths is 30 hundredths and 5 hundredths or 3 tenths and 5 hundredths.

©Curriculum Associates, LLC   Copying is not permitted

CONNECT IT

Now you will use the problem from the previous page to help you understand how to write a mixed number given in word form as a decimal in standard form. *(decimal point)*

1 Compare the mixed-number and the place-value representations of *one and sixteen thousandths*. How does each model show the number of whole seconds?

$1 \frac{16}{100}$ *By putting the whole number before the point representing the whole second or using and after the number of whole seconds.*

2 Compare the expanded form and the place-value representations of *one and sixteenth thousandths*. How does each model show the fractional part of a second?

By putting in after the whole second as a decimal or a fraction.

3 How can you write *one and sixteen thousandths* as a decimal? .... 1.016 ....

1.016

4 How can you write *two and thirty-five hundredths* as a decimal? ...... 2.35/ ....

2.

5 Explain how you can write the standard form of a decimal given in word form.

I can write the standard form of a decimal given in word form by knowing the if it has a a number in the ones place it would be call normal and when you read the point you read as an and. After that you read the number normal but, depending where it ends you add the position name to the number.

6 **REFLECT**

Look back at your **Try It**, strategies by classmates, and **Model Its**. Which models or strategies do you like best for writing the standard form of a mixed number given in word form? Explain.

.... 1. ....

APPLY IT

Use what you just learned to solve these problems.

7 What decimal represents *ten and seventy-five hundredths*? Show your work.

Solution 10.75Ø (make sure you end in the hundredths place

8 A number is written in expanded form as $9 \times 1{,}000 + 6 \times 1 + 3 \times \frac{1}{10} + 8 \times \frac{1}{1{,}000}$. What decimal represents the number? Show your work.

$$9 \times 1{,}000 + 6 \times 1 + 3 \times \frac{1}{10} + 8 \times \frac{1}{1{,}000}$$

$$9{,}000 \qquad + 6 \qquad + \frac{3}{10} \text{ or } \frac{30}{100} + \frac{8}{1{,}000}$$

$$\frac{300}{1{,}000}$$

$$9000 + 6 + \left(\frac{300}{1000} + \frac{8}{1000}\right) \frac{308}{1000}$$

Solution 9006.308

$$9006 + \frac{308}{1000}$$

$$9006 \frac{308}{1000}$$

9 Which decimal represents *six and fifty-four thousandths*?

Ⓐ 60.54

Ⓑ 6.540

Ⓒ 6.054

Ⓓ 0.654

9006.308

©Curriculum Associates, LLC   Copying is not permitted

Compare and Round Decimals

Dear Family,

This week your child is learning to compare and round decimals.

One way to compare decimals is to use a place-value chart. For example, compare 7.033 and 7.02. Write a 0 in the thousandths column for 7.02. Start by comparing the ones.

Ones	.	Tenths	Hundredths	Thousandths
7	.	0	3	3
7	.	0	2	0

$$7 = 7 \qquad 0 = 0 \qquad 3 > 2$$

The ones digits are the same. The tenths digits are the same.
3 hundredths > 2 hundredths. So, 7.033 > 7.02.

Another way to compare decimals is to write them as mixed numbers. Write the fractions with like denominators.

$$7.033 = 7\frac{33}{1,000} \qquad\qquad 7.02 = 7\frac{2}{100} = 7\frac{20}{1,000}$$

$$7\frac{33}{1,000} > 7\frac{20}{1,000}$$

So, 7.033 > 7.02.

Your child is also learning to round decimals using a number line.
The number line shows that 0.042 is closer to 0.04 than to 0.05.

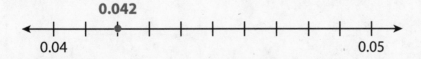

0.042 rounded to the nearest hundredth is 0.04.

Invite your child to share what he or she knows about comparing and rounding decimals by doing the following activity together.

ACTIVITY COMPARE DECIMALS

Do this activity with your child to compare decimals.

Work with your child to find real-world examples that involve comparing decimals.

- Look around the house or through fliers for at least eight numbers that involve a decimal. The wrappers or labels on household items usually show a number. Make a list of the decimals as you find them. You do not need to write the units.

- Examples: a 3.17-ounce bar of soap, an 8.5-ounce bottle of lotion, a 7.4-ounce box of snack bars, a 7.9-ounce box of crackers.

- Take turns. One person marks two numbers for the other person to compare. Make a place-value chart like the one on the first page of this letter if needed. Circle the greater decimal.

- Challenge! After you have finished the activity, you should now have four sets of decimal numbers with the greater decimal circled. Can you determine the greatest decimal of those four decimals?

©Curriculum Associates, LLC   Copying is not permitted

Explore Comparing and Rounding Decimals

You already know how to compare and round whole numbers. In this lesson, you will use place-value understanding to compare and round decimals. Use what you know to try to solve the problem below.

Florida Standards

5.NBT.1.3b Compare two decimals to thousandths based on meanings of the digits in each place, using >, =, and < symbols to record the results of comparisons.

5.NBT.1.4 Use place value understanding to round decimals to any place.

> **Grace chooses one red and one blue button from her button collection. The blue button is 1.2 centimeters wide and the red button is 1.08 centimeters wide. Which button is wider?**

TRY IT

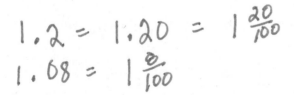

Ones	Decimal	Tenths	Hundredth
1	.	2	
1	.	0	8

Blue is wider

$$1.2 = 1.20 = 1\frac{20}{100}$$
$$1.08 = 1\frac{8}{100}$$

🧰 **Math Toolkit**
- base-ten blocks
- base-ten grid paper
- decimal grids
- place-value charts
- number lines

DISCUSS IT

Ask your partner: How did you get started?

Tell your partner: I started by . . .

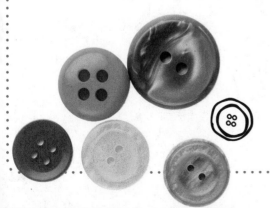

CONNECT IT

① LOOK BACK

Which button is wider? Use the *greater than* symbol (>) or the *less than* symbol (<) to write an **inequality** statement that compares the widths of the red and blue buttons Grace chose from her collection.

$$1.2 > 1.08$$

② LOOK AHEAD

You can use decimal comparisons to help you round decimals to a given place value. Rounding decimals is similar to rounding whole numbers.

a. A number line can be a useful tool for rounding. Place and label the numbers 1.3 and 1.8 on the number line below.

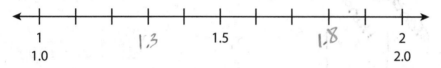

1   1.3   1.5   1.8   2
1.0   2.0

b. What is 1.3 rounded to the nearest whole number? Explain how you know.

1 because is not 5 or above

c. What is 1.8 rounded to the nearest whole number? Explain how you know.

2

d. What is 1.5 rounded to the nearest whole number? Explain how you know.

2

③ REFLECT

How is rounding decimals like rounding whole numbers?

The rules I used to round hole numbers are the same for decimals.

©Curriculum Associates, LLC   Copying is not permitted

Develop Comparing Decimals

Read and try to solve the problem below.

Gary and Melissa compare the distances they bike each morning to get to school.

- Gary bikes 3.275 kilometers.

- Melissa bikes 3.24 kilometers.

Who bikes farther to get to school?

TRY IT

 **Math Toolkit**
- place-value charts
- number lines
- base-ten grid paper

	ones	Decimal	Tenths	Hundredths	thousandths
Gary	3	.	2	7	5
Melissa	3	.	2	4	0

Gary bikes farther to school because, he has the 7 in the hundredths place.

$$Gary = 3\frac{275}{1000}$$
$$Melissa = 3\frac{240}{1000}$$

DISCUSS IT

Ask your partner: Can you explain that again?

Tell your partner: I knew ... so I ...

Explore different ways to understand comparing decimals.

> **Gary and Melissa compare the distances they bike each morning to get to school.**
>
> • **Gary bikes 3.275 kilometers.**
>
> • **Melissa bikes 3.24 kilometers.**
>
> **Who bikes farther to get to school?**

MODEL IT
Express the two distances as mixed numbers with like denominators.

Gary: $3.275 = 3\frac{275}{1,000}$ 　　　 Melissa: $3.24 = 3\frac{24}{100}$

$$= 3\frac{240}{1,000}$$

You can now compare $3\frac{275}{1,000}$ to $3\frac{240}{1,000}$.

MODEL IT
Write the distances in a place-value chart.

	Ones	.	Tenths	Hundredths	Thousandths
Gary	3	.	2	7	5
Melissa	3	.	2	4	0

Gary bikes 3,275 thousandths kilometers to get to school.
Melissa bikes 3,240 thousandths kilometers to get to school.

You can use the chart to compare place values starting with the ones.

 ©Curriculum Associates, LLC Copying is not permitted

CONNECT IT

Now you will use the problem from the previous page to help you understand how to compare decimals.

1 Both **Model Its** change the way the fractional part or decimal part of 3.24 is represented. What is the same about how the denominator of the fraction and the place value of the decimal change?

2 What is the same about how the numerator of the fraction and the digits to the right of the decimal point change?

3 How does rewriting the fractional part or decimal part of 3.24 make it easier to compare 3.24 to 3.275?

4 Write an inequality statement using the symbol > to compare the distances Gary and Melissa bike. Who bikes farther to school?

5 Look at the place-value chart in the second **Model It**. What is the greatest place value for which the numbers 3.275 and 3.24 have different digits? ....

How can you use this place value to show that Gary bikes farther?

6 REFLECT

Look back at your **Try It**, strategies by classmates, and **Model Its**. Which models or strategies do you like best for comparing decimals? Explain.

....

....

....

APPLY IT

Use what you just learned to solve these problems.

7 On the same day, Brayden recorded 1.46 inches of rain at his house and Kayla recorded 1.62 inches of rain at her house. Who recorded fewer inches of rain at their house that day? Show your work.

$$B\ 1.46 \qquad 1\frac{46}{100} \qquad \frac{46}{100} < \frac{62}{100}$$
$$K\ 1.62 \qquad 1\frac{62}{100}$$

Solution ..Brayden...

8 Heather's rabbit has a mass of 5.190 kilograms. Jelani's rabbit has a mass of 5.195 kilograms. Write an inequality statement comparing the masses of the rabbits. Whose rabbit has the greater mass? Show your work.

$$H\ 5.190 \qquad 5.190 < 5.195$$
$$J\ 5.195$$

Solution ..Jelani's...

9 Select all the decimals that are greater than 715.148 and also less than 715.35.

Ⓐ 715.340

Ⓑ 715.4

Ⓒ 714.156

Ⓓ 715.075

Ⓔ 715.28

©Curriculum Associates, LLC   Copying is not permitted

Develop Rounding Decimals

Read and try to solve the problem below.

> Tyson runs in a 100-meter race at a track meet.
> One stopwatch shows his time as 11.25 seconds.
> Another stopwatch shows his time as 11.245 seconds.
> Round each time to the nearest tenth of a second.

TRY IT

Tens	ones	decimal	tenths	hundredths	Thousandths	
1	1	.	2	5	0	= 11.300
1	1	.	2	4	5	= 11.200

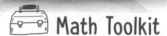
Math Toolkit
- place-value charts
- number lines
- base-ten grid paper

DISCUSS IT

Ask your partner: Do you agree with me? Why or why not?

Tell your partner: I agree with you about ... because ...

Explore ways to understand rounding decimals.

> **Tyson runs in a 100-meter race at a track meet. One stopwatch shows his time as 11.25 seconds. Another stopwatch shows his time as 11.245 seconds. Round each time to the nearest tenth of a second.**

PICTURE IT

You can place each number on a number line to see its relationship to nearby tenths.

11.25 is exactly halfway between **11.2** and **11.3**.

You can locate **11.245** between **11.24** and **11.25**. **11.245** is less than halfway between **11.2** and **11.3**.

MODEL IT

You can use a place-value chart to compare a decimal to nearby tenths.

Tens	Ones	.	Tenths	Hundredths
1	1	.	2	0
1	1	.	2	5
1	1	.	3	0

> **25** hundredths is halfway between **20** hundredths and **30** hundredths.

When you are rounding to the nearest tenth, you do not need to look at the thousandths place.

Tens	Ones	.	Tenths	Hundredths	Thousandths
1	1	.	2	0	0
1	1	.	2	4	5
1	1	.	3	0	0

> **24** hundredths is closer to **20** hundredths than it is to **30** hundredths.

©Curriculum Associates, LLC Copying is not permitted

CONNECT IT

Now you will use the problem from the previous page to help you understand how to round decimals.

1 Look at **Picture It** and **Model It**. Why do the number lines and place-value charts start at 11.2 and end at 11.3?

Because 11.25 was between those two numbers

2 How do you know 11.25 is located at the halfway point between 11.2 and 11.3?

3 What are 11.25 and 11.245 rounded to the nearest tenth? Use the number line to support your answers.

$$11.25 \; =$$
$$11.245 \; =$$

4 How do the place-value charts help you see that 11.245 is closer to 11.2 than to 11.3?

5 If you are rounding to the nearest tenth, what place value do you look at to decide how to round the number? ....

6 Explain how you would round a decimal to the nearest hundredth.

7 REFLECT

Look back at your **Try It**, strategies by classmates, **Picture It** and **Model It**. Which models or strategies do you like best for rounding decimals? Explain.

....

....

....

Lesson 9 Compare and Round Decimals   **179**

APPLY IT

Use what you just learned to solve these problems.

8 Belinda paid $108.34 for groceries. Rounded to the nearest dollar, how much did Belinda pay for groceries? Show your work.

$$\$108.34$$

Solution $\$108$

9 A dropper holds 0.817 milliliter of fluid. What is this amount rounded to the nearest hundredth? Show your work.

$$0.8\overset{2}{1}7$$

Solution 0.820 milliliters

10 Which decimals have been rounded correctly to the nearest tenth?

Ⓐ 7.834 rounded to 7.83 $7.834 = 7.8$

Ⓑ 10.056 rounded to 10.1 $10.056 = 10.1$

Ⓒ 0.651 rounded to 0.65 $0.651 = 0.70$

Ⓓ 203.209 rounded to 203.2 $203.209 = 203.2$

Ⓔ 115.007 rounded to 120.10 $115.007 = 115.0$

＊ If we are rounding to the tenths place = your answer will end @ tenths place

©Curriculum Associates, LLC   Copying is not permitted

Add Decimals

Dear Family,

This week your child is learning to add decimals.

The strategies you use to add whole numbers can also be used to add decimals. You might use place-value understanding, decimal models, or number properties that allow you to break apart numbers and add numbers in different orders.

For example, you can add 4.38 and 0.6 by lining the numbers up by place value.

	Ones	.	Tenths	Hundredths
	4	.	3	8
+	0	.	6	0
	4	.	9	8

6 tenths is the same as 60 hundredths!

So, 4.38 + 0.6 = 4.98.

You can also use concrete models, such as decimal grids, to add **4.38** and **0.6**. Each grid of 100 squares represents one whole.

4   + 0.38   + 0.6   = 4.98

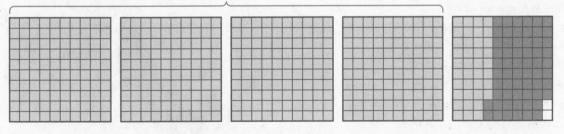

Invite your child to share what he or she knows about adding decimals by doing the following activity together.

Lesson 10 Add Decimals   **187**

ACTIVITY ADDING DECIMALS

Do this activity with your child to add decimals.

Materials calculator (optional)

Work with your child to make up and solve real-world problems involving addition of decimals.

- Take turns finding or making up some stories with decimal numbers. Include a decimal addition problem for the other person to solve.

- First, try to solve the problems with paper and pencil. Then check your answers with a calculator.

- Here are some examples of problems you might solve:

  - Gavin caught two fish on a camping trip. The masses of the fish are 12.25 kilograms and 7.4 kilograms. What is the total mass of the fish Gavin caught?

  - Angelique jumped forward 1.83 meters. Then she jumped forward another 1.72 meters. What is the total distance Angelique jumped?

- Be on the lookout for other real-world examples of adding decimals. For example, a grocery receipt shows decimal addition. Challenge your child to estimate the sum, then look at the receipt to check.

©Curriculum Associates, LLC   Copying is not permitted

Explore **Adding Decimals**

You know how to add whole numbers by adding the values of digits with the same place value. Now you will learn to add decimals. Use what you know to try to solve the problem below.

Florida Standards

5.NBT.2.7 Add, subtract, multiply, and divide decimals to hundredths, using concrete models or drawings and strategies based on place value, properties of operations, and/or the relationship between addition and subtraction; relate the strategy to a written method and explain the reasoning used.

Sabrina and Christie are running in a relay. Sabrina runs 100 meters in 13.6 seconds. Christie runs the same distance in 12.2 seconds. What is their total time?

TRY IT

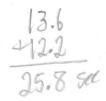
$$
\begin{array}{r}
13.6 \\
+12.2 \\
\hline
25.8 \text{ sec}
\end{array}
$$

 Math Toolkit
- base-ten blocks
- base-ten grid paper
- decimal grids
- number lines
- place-value charts

DISCUSS IT

Ask your partner: How did you get started?

Tell your partner: I started by . . .

CONNECT IT

1 LOOK BACK

Explain how you can find Sabrina and Christie's total time.

2 LOOK AHEAD

You can add decimals in different ways, just like you can add whole numbers in different ways. Think about the problem 32.14 + 17.5.

a. Write the problem in the place-value chart below and find the sum.

	Tens	Ones	.	Tenths	Hundredths
			.		
+			.		
			.		

How did the place-value chart help you add?

b. Use expanded form to break apart each addend by place value.

Break apart 32.14: ....

Break apart 17.5: ....

Find the sum 32.14 + 17.5 by adding the parts in any order.

3 REFLECT

How is adding decimals like adding whole numbers?

....

....

....

 ©Curriculum Associates, LLC Copying is not permitted

Prepare for Adding Decimals

1   Think about what you know about breaking apart numbers with addition. Fill in each box. Use words, numbers, and pictures. Show as many ideas as you can.

What Is It?	What I Know About It

break apart a decimal

Examples	Examples	Examples

2   Write the problem 37.2 + 1.6 in the place-value chart and find the sum.

How did the place-value chart help you add?

Tens	Ones	.	Tenths
		.	
+		.	
		.	

3 Solve the problem. Show your work.

Manny and Soo are paired up in a competition where they take turns stacking blocks to make a tower. Manny's part of the tower is 15.36 inches tall, and Soo's part of the tower is 13.5 inches tall. How tall is the tower?

4 Check your answer. Show your work.

©Curriculum Associates, LLC   Copying is not permitted

Develop Adding Decimals

Read and try to solve the problem below.

> From his home, Tim rides the bus 3.82 miles. Then he walks 0.4 mile from the bus stop to school. How many miles does Tim travel from home to school?

TRY IT

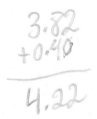

$$\begin{array}{r} 3.82 \\ +\ 0.40 \\ \hline 4.22 \end{array}$$

 **Math Toolkit**
- base-ten blocks
- base-ten grid paper
- decimal grids
- number lines
- place-value charts

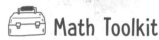

DISCUSS IT

Ask your partner: Can you explain that again?

Tell your partner: I knew . . . so I . . .

©Curriculum Associates, LLC   Copying is not permitted

Explore different ways to understand adding decimals.

From his home, Tim rides the bus 3.82 miles. Then he walks 0.4 mile from the bus stop to school. How many miles does Tim travel from home to school?

PICTURE IT

You can picture adding two decimals on a number line.

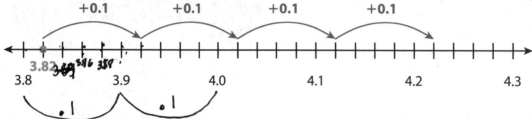

Starting at 3.82, you can make 4 jumps of 0.1 to the right to show the sum of 3.82 and 0.4.

MODEL IT

You can use a place-value chart to help you understand how to add decimals.

	Ones	.	Tenths	Hundredths
Bus ride	3	.	8	2
Bus stop to school	0	.	4	0

$\frac{4}{10}$ is equivalent to $\frac{40}{100}$, so you can write a 0 in the hundredths column.

The sum is 3 ones + 12 tenths + 2 hundredths.

   ©Curriculum Associates, LLC   Copying is not permitted

CONNECT IT

Now you will use the problem from the previous page to help you understand how to add decimals.

1 How can you use the number line in **Picture It** to figure out how many miles Tim travels from home to school?

2 Look at **Model It**. What is another way to express 12 tenths? ....

What is another way to express the sum? ....

What is this sum in decimal form? ....

3 You can add the decimals without a place-value chart by stacking them vertically. Why do you align the 8 in 3.82 with the 4 in 0.40?

$$\begin{array}{r} 3.82 \\ + \ 0.40 \\ \hline \end{array}$$

4 The addition problem to the right is partially completed. Explain why there is a 1 above the ones place. Then complete the sum.

$$\begin{array}{r} {}^{1}3.82 \\ + \ 0.40 \\ \hline \boxed{}.22 \end{array}$$

5 Explain how to add decimals.

6 REFLECT

Look back at your **Try It**, strategies by classmates, and **Picture It** and **Model It**. Which models or strategies do you like best for adding decimals? Explain.

....

....

....

....

Lesson 10 Add Decimals   **195**

APPLY IT

Use what you just learned to solve these problems.

7 Yana makes a trail mix with 6.25 ounces of dried fruit and 1.8 ounces of sunflower seeds. How many ounces of trail mix does Yana make? Show your work.

Solution ....

8 What is the value of the expression $2.25 + 63.05 + 0.6$? First, estimate the sum. Then find an exact answer. Show your work.

Solution ....

9 Jorge spends $42.75 on a new jacket and $88.30 on a pair of running shoes. How much money does he spend in all? Show your work.

Solution ....

©Curriculum Associates, LLC   Copying is not permitted

Subtract Decimals

Dear Family,

This week your child is learning to subtract decimals.

Your child can use what he or she knows about subtracting whole numbers to subtract decimals.

Strategies for subtraction include place-value understanding, drawing decimal models or number lines, using number properties that allow you to break apart numbers, and using the relationship between addition and subtraction.

For example, you can subtract 0.32 from 3.48 by lining up numbers by place value.

	Ones	.	Tenths	Hundredths
	3	.	4	8
−	0	.	3	2
	3	.	1	6

You can also subtract 0.32 from 3.48 on a number line by breaking apart 0.32 into 0.3 and 0.02 and subtracting in parts.

On the number line below, the tick marks are 0.02 (2 hundredths) of a unit apart, so each hop of 5 tick marks represents subtracting 0.1. Starting at **3.48**, you can subtract 0.1 three times and then subtract 0.02. So, **3.48** − **0.32** = **3.16**.

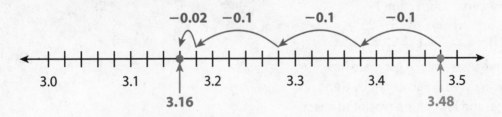

Invite your child to share what he or she knows about subtracting decimals by doing the following activity together.

ACTIVITY SUBTRACTING DECIMALS

Do this activity with your child to subtract decimals.

Materials calculator (optional)

Work with your child to make up and solve real-world problems involving subtraction of decimals.

- Take turns finding or making up some stories with decimal numbers. Include a decimal subtraction problem for the other person to solve.

- First, try to solve the problems with paper and pencil. Then check your answers with a calculator.

- Here are some examples:

  - A large fish measured 284.56 centimeters long. At one time, the world's longest goldfish was 47.4 centimeters long. What is the difference in length between the two fish?

  - A dog jumped 1.13 meters, and its human owner jumped 1.21 meters. How much further did the owner jump than the dog?

- Be on the lookout for other real-world examples of subtracting decimals. For example, a grocery receipt shows decimal subtraction when coupons are used to reduce the price of certain items. Challenge your child to estimate how much you saved on groceries by using coupons, and look at the receipt to check.

©Curriculum Associates, LLC   Copying is not permitted

Explore Subtracting Decimals

You have learned how to add decimals by adding the values of the digits with the same place values. Now you will learn how to subtract decimals. Use what you know to try to solve the problem below.

The mass of a female hummingbird is 4.5 grams. The mass of a male hummingbird is 3.2 grams. What is the difference between the masses of the female and male hummingbirds?

Florida Standards

5.NBT.2.7 Add, subtract, multiply, and divide decimals to hundredths, using concrete models or drawings and strategies based on place value, properties of operations, and/or the relationship between addition and subtraction; relate the strategy to a written method and explain the reasoning used.

TRY IT

female
4.5

male 3.2

$$
\begin{array}{r}
4.5 \\
-3.2 \\
\hline
1.3\ grams
\end{array}
$$

 **Math Toolkit**
- base-ten blocks
- base-ten grid paper
- decimal grids
- number lines
- place-value charts

 **DISCUSS IT**

Ask your partner: Can you explain that again?

Tell your partner: I started by . . .

CONNECT IT

1 LOOK BACK

Explain how you can find the difference between the masses of the female and male hummingbirds.

2 LOOK AHEAD

You can subtract decimals in different ways just like you can subtract whole numbers in different ways. Think about the problem 2.98 − 2.56.

a. Write the problem in the place-value chart below and find the difference.

Ones	.	Tenths	Hundredths
2	.	9	8
− 2	.	5	6
0	.	4	2

b. You can also find the difference using an adding on strategy. Use the numbers above the jump arrows on the number line to find the difference **2.98 − 2.56**.

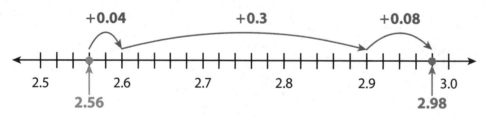

2.98 − 2.56 = ...0.04.... + ...0.3...... + ...0.08.... = ...0.42......

3 REFLECT

How is subtracting decimals like subtracting whole numbers?

....

....

....

©Curriculum Associates, LLC   Copying is not permitted

Develop Subtracting Decimals to Hundredths

Read and try to solve the problem below.

> Marty eats 2.05 ounces of cheese from a 4.6-ounce
> block of cheddar cheese. How many ounces of
> cheddar cheese are left?

TRY IT

 **Math Toolkit**
- base-ten blocks
- base-ten grid paper
- decimal grids
- number lines
- place-value charts

$$4.\overset{5}{\cancel{6}}\overset{1}{0}$$
$$-2.05$$
$$\overline{2.55}$$

$4.6 - 2.05 =$

$$4\tfrac{6}{10} - 2\tfrac{5}{100}$$

$$\downarrow \qquad\qquad \downarrow$$

$$4\tfrac{60}{100} - 2\tfrac{5}{100}$$

$$2\tfrac{55}{100}$$

$$2.55$$

DISCUSS IT

Ask your partner: How did you get started?

Tell your partner: The strategy I used to find the answer was . . .

©Curriculum Associates, LLC   Copying is not permitted

Explore different ways to understand subtracting decimals.

> **Marty eats 2.05 ounces of cheese from a 4.6-ounce block of cheddar cheese. How many ounces of cheddar cheese are left?**

PICTURE IT

You can subtract decimals using base-ten models.

Model 4 wholes and 6 tenths.

6 tenths = 60 hundredths

Cross out 2 wholes and 5 hundredths.

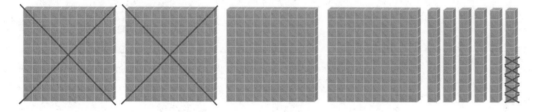

MODEL IT

You can subtract decimals using a place-value chart.

Using a place-value chart helps you make sure the place values are lined up correctly.

	Ones	.	Tenths	Hundredths
Original amount	4	.	6	0
Amount eaten	2	.	0	5

> $\frac{6}{10}$ is equivalent to $\frac{60}{100}$, so you can write a 0 in the hundredths column.

 ©Curriculum Associates, LLC Copying is not permitted

CONNECT IT

Now you will use the problem from the previous page to help you understand how to subtract decimals.

1 Look at the base-ten models in **Picture It**. Explain why parts of the models are crossed out.

2 According to **Picture It**, how many ounces of cheese are left? ....

3 Look at the place-value chart in **Model It**. You can subtract the decimals without a place-value chart by stacking them vertically. Line up the decimal points to keep track of place values.

$$\begin{array}{r} 4.60 \\ -\ 2.05 \end{array}$$

Explain why you cannot subtract the 5 from the 6 when finding the difference.

4 Another way to express 6 tenths is .... tenths + 10 hundredths.

So you can rewrite the problem as shown at the right.

$$\begin{array}{r} \overset{5\ 10}{4.\cancel{6}0} \\ -\ 2.05 \\ \hline \boxed{} \end{array}$$

Complete the subtraction. There are .... ounces of cheese left.

5 Explain how to subtract two decimals.

6 REFLECT

Look back at your **Try It**, strategies by classmates, and **Picture It** and **Model It**. Which models or strategies do you like best for subtracting decimals? Explain.

....

....

....

....

©Curriculum Associates, LLC   Copying is not permitted

APPLY IT

Use what you just learned to solve these problems.

7 Anya has $3.07 in her change purse. She spends $1.15 on snacks at the vending machine. How much money does Anya have left? Show your work.

$$
\begin{array}{r}
2\overset{1}{\cancel{3}}.07 \\
-1.15 \\
+1.92 \\
\hline
3.07
\end{array}
$$

Solution 1.92

8 Destiny is sending a box to a friend. The box weighs 23.5 pounds. Destiny removes a 4.47-pound book to decrease the shipping cost. What is the new weight of the box? Show your work.

$$
\begin{array}{r}
2\overset{1}{3}.\overset{4}{\cancel{5}}\overset{1}{0} \\
-4.47 \\
\hline
19.03
\end{array}
$$

19.03

19 and 3 hundredths

Solution 19.03

9 What is 241.3 − 81.55?

Ⓐ 150.85

Ⓑ 169.75

$$
\begin{array}{r}
2\overset{3}{4}\overset{0}{1}.\overset{12}{3}0 \\
-81.55 \\
\hline
159.75
\end{array}
$$

Ⓒ 159.85

Ⓓ 159.75

©Curriculum Associates, LLC   Copying is not permitted

Develop Adding On to Subtract

Read and try to solve the problem below.

> Galen can reach up to a height of 1.87 meters while standing flat on
> the ground. His father can reach a height of 2.56 meters. How much
> higher than Galen can Galen's father reach? Use addition to help solve
> the problem.

TRY IT

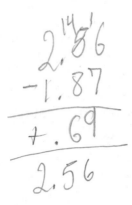

$$
\begin{array}{r}
2.\overset{14}{\cancel{5}}\overset{1}{\cancel{6}} \\
-1.87 \\
\hline
+.69 \\
\hline
2.56
\end{array}
$$

 **Math Toolkit**
- base-ten blocks
- base-ten grid paper
- decimal grids
- number lines
- place-value charts

DISCUSS IT

Ask your partner: Why did
you choose that strategy?

Tell your partner: A model
I used was . . . It helped
me . . .

Explore ways to understand using the relationship between addition and subtraction to subtract decimals.

> Galen can reach up to a height of 1.87 meters while standing flat on the ground. His father can reach a height of 2.56 meters. How much higher than Galen can Galen's father reach? Use addition to help solve the problem.

PICTURE IT

You can draw a bar model to understand the problem.

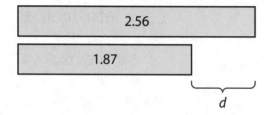

Use the bar model to write equations that represent the problem.

Subtraction equation: $2.56 - 1.87 = d$

Related addition equation: $1.87 + d = 2.56$

MODEL IT

You can use a number line to model adding on to find a difference.

Start at **1.87** on the number line and add on to get to **2.56**.

Find the numbers that you add to get to an easier number.

$1.87 + 0.03 = 1.90$ ◀— Add on **3 hundredths** to get to the next tenth.

$1.90 + 0.1 = 2.00$ ◀— Add on **1 tenth** to get to the next whole number.

$2.00 + 0.56 = 2.56$ ◀— Add on **56 hundredths** to get to the total, 2.56.

©Curriculum Associates, LLC   Copying is not permitted

CONNECT IT

Now you will use the problem from the previous page to understand how to use the relationship between addition and subtraction to subtract decimals.

1 Look at the bar model and the addition and subtraction equations in **Picture It**. What does the letter *d* represent?

What do the numbers 2.56 and 1.87 represent?

2 Look at the number line in **Model It**. Why does the number line start at 1.87?

3 How can you use the jump numbers above the number line to find the value of *d*?

How much higher can Galen's father reach? ....

4 How can addition help you subtract decimals?

5 REFLECT

Look back at your **Try It**, strategies by classmates, and **Picture It** and **Model It**. Which models or strategies do you like best for using addition to help you subtract decimals? Explain.

....

....

....

APPLY IT

Use what you just learned to solve these problems.

6 At a swim meet, Quinn's time for the 50-meter freestyle event was 25.3 seconds. His sister, Darby, swam the same event in 24.85 seconds. How much faster did Darby swim 50 meters than Quinn? Show your work.

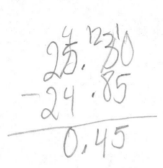

$$
\begin{array}{r}
25.\overset{4}{\cancel{3}}\overset{12}{\cancel{3}}\overset{1}{0} \\
-24.85 \\
\hline
0.45
\end{array}
$$

Solution 45

7 Tamika has two guinea pigs for pets. Smokey weighs 39.73 ounces and Tito weighs 42.25 ounces. How much more does Tito weigh than Smokey? Show how to solve the problem by adding on.

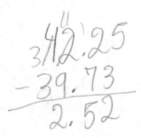

$$
\begin{array}{r}
3\overset{4}{\cancel{4}}2.25 \\
-39.73 \\
\hline
2.52
\end{array}
$$

Solution 2.52 ounces

8 Which equation can you use to find 55.15 − 47.29?

  Ⓐ 47.29 + n = 55.15

  Ⓒ n = 47.29 + 55.15

55.15
47

  Ⓑ 55.15 + n = 47.29

  Ⓓ 47.29 = (55.1 + 0.5) − n

©Curriculum Associates, LLC   Copying is not permitted

Add Fractions

Dear Family,

This week your child is learning to add fractions with unlike denominators.

Here is how a model can show fraction addition, such as $1\frac{3}{5} + \frac{1}{3}$.

$$1\frac{3}{5} \quad + \quad \frac{1}{3}$$

> The denominators, 5 and 3, tell how many equal parts are in the whole. 5 and 3 are **unlike denominators**.

The parts of the whole are different sizes, thirds and fifths. You cannot add different-size parts. You need to divide the model to show equal-size parts, fifteenths.

$$1\frac{3}{5} = 1\frac{9}{15} \quad + \quad \frac{1}{3} = \frac{5}{15}$$

> The denominator, 15, tells that there are 15 equal parts in the whole. So, 15 and 15 are **like denominators**.

Then add. $1\frac{3}{5} + \frac{1}{3} = 1\frac{9}{15} + \frac{5}{15} = 1\frac{14}{15}$

Some other ways your child can think about adding fractions are to use a number line model or to use multiplication to replace the given fractions with equivalent fractions that have the same denominator.

Invite your child to share what he or she knows about adding fractions by doing the following activity together.

ACTIVITY ADDING FRACTIONS

Do this activity with your child to add fractions.

Work together with your child to solve real-world problems about adding fractions.

- Suppose you want to make some healthy snacks and you have $\frac{7}{8}$ cup of cream cheese and $\frac{3}{4}$ cup raisins.

- Look at the two recipes below. Add fractions to decide if there is enough cream cheese and raisins to make both recipes.

Recipe
Recipe for Creamed Crackers

Ingredients:
12 crackers
(any variety)

$\frac{1}{2}$ cup cream cheese

$\frac{1}{4}$ cup raisins

Directions:
Spread cream cheese evenly on crackers.

Sprinkle with raisins.

Recipe
Recipe for Celery Logs

Ingredients:
6 two-inch pieces of celery

$\frac{1}{3}$ cup cream cheese

$\frac{1}{8}$ cup raisins

Directions:
Spread cream cheese evenly on celery.

Sprinkle with raisins.

©Curriculum Associates, LLC   Copying is not permitted

Explore Adding Fractions

You know how to add fractions with like denominators. Now you will learn how to add fractions with unlike denominators. Use what you know to try to solve the problem below.

> Emiliano needs $\frac{1}{2}$ stick of butter to make corn bread. He also needs $\frac{1}{4}$ stick of butter to make apple muffins. What fraction of a stick of butter does he need in all?

Florida Standards

5.NF.1.1 Add and subtract fractions with unlike denominators (including mixed numbers) by replacing given fractions with equivalent fractions in such a way as to produce an equivalent sum or difference of fractions with like denominators.

5.NF.1.2

TRY IT

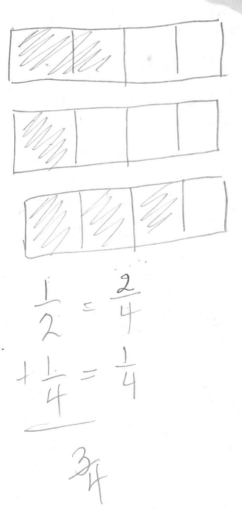

$$2 = 2, \boxed{4}, 6, 8$$
$$4 = \boxed{4}, 8, 12$$

$$\frac{1}{2} = \frac{2}{4}$$
$$+ \frac{1}{4} = \frac{1}{4}$$
$$\overline{}$$
$$\frac{3}{4}$$

Math Toolkit
- fraction tiles
- fraction circles
- fraction bars
- grid paper
- number lines

DISCUSS IT

Ask your partner: Why did you choose that strategy?

Tell your partner: I knew . . . so I . . .

CONNECT IT

1 LOOK BACK

Explain how you found how much butter Emiliano needs.

2 LOOK AHEAD

Before adding fractions, the fractions must have the same-size parts of a whole. You can use what you know about multiples and equivalent fractions to find a **common denominator** for fractions that have unlike denominators.

a. Use the fractions $\frac{1}{2}$ and $\frac{1}{3}$. Write the next four multiples of each denominator. Then circle the multiple that 2 and 3 have in common.

Multiples of 2: 2, 4 , ⑥ , 8 , 10

Multiples of 3: 3, ⑥ , 9 , 12 , 15

b. Complete the models and equations to show equivalent fractions for $\frac{1}{2}$ and $\frac{1}{3}$ using the common multiple as the common denominator.

$$\frac{1}{2} = \frac{3}{6} \qquad \frac{1}{3} = \frac{2}{6}$$

c. Use the equivalent fractions to add. $\quad \frac{1}{2} + \frac{1}{3} = \frac{3}{6} + \frac{2}{6} = \frac{5}{6}$

3 REFLECT

What equivalent fractions could you write to add $\frac{1}{2}$ and $\frac{2}{3}$? Explain.

Multiples ② 2, 4, ⑥, 8
③ 3, ⑥, 9, 12

$$\frac{1}{2} = \frac{3}{6}$$

$$\frac{2}{3} = \frac{4}{6}$$

©Curriculum Associates, LLC Copying is not permitted

Develop Adding Fractions with Unlike Denominators

Read and try to solve the problem below.

Maggie is making a juice mix using
$\frac{1}{2}$ cup cranberry juice and $\frac{4}{5}$ cup apple juice.
How many cups of juice does she make?

TRY IT

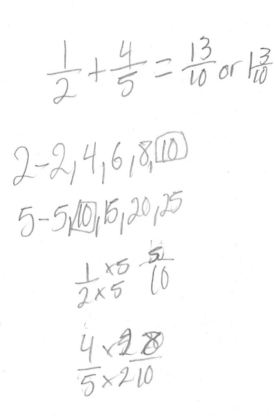

$$\frac{1}{2} + \frac{4}{5} = \frac{13}{10} \text{ or } 1\frac{3}{10}$$

$2 - 2, 4, 6, 8, \boxed{10}$

$5 - 5, \cancel{10}, 15, 20, 25$

$\frac{1 \times 5}{2 \times 5} \quad \frac{5}{10}$

$\frac{4 \times 2}{5 \times 2} \quad \frac{8}{10}$

 Math Toolkit
- fraction tiles
- fraction circles
- fractions bars
- grid paper
- number lines

DISCUSS IT

Ask your partner: Do you agree with me? Why or why not?

Tell your partner: I disagree with this part because . . .

©Curriculum Associates, LLC Copying is not permitted

Explore different ways to understand adding fractions with unlike denominators.

> Maggie is making a juice mix using $\frac{1}{2}$ cup cranberry juice and $\frac{4}{5}$ cup apple juice. How many cups of juice does she make?

PICTURE IT

You can picture the fractions in the problem using fraction bars.

The fraction bars are divided into halves and fifths.

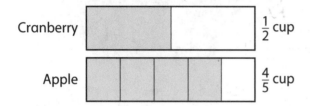

Cranberry $\frac{1}{2}$ cup

Apple $\frac{4}{5}$ cup

Both fraction bars need to be divided into same-size parts.

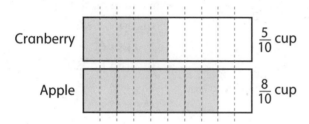

Cranberry $\frac{5}{10}$ cup

Apple $\frac{8}{10}$ cup

Now you can add equivalent fractions.

MODEL IT

You can model the problem with an equation.

Replace the fractions $\frac{1}{2}$ and $\frac{4}{5}$ with equivalent fractions with a common denominator.

$$\frac{1}{2} = \frac{1 \times 5}{2 \times 5} = \frac{5}{10} \text{ and}$$

$$\frac{4}{5} = \frac{4 \times 2}{5 \times 2} = \frac{8}{10}$$

So, $\frac{1}{2} + \frac{4}{5} = \frac{5}{10} + \frac{8}{10}$.

    ©Curriculum Associates, LLC   Copying is not permitted

CONNECT IT

Now you will use the problem from the previous page to help you understand how to add any two fractions with unlike denominators.

1 Explain why both fraction bars in **Picture It** are divided into 10 equal pieces.

2 Write the total amount of juice Maggie makes as a fraction. ....$\frac{13}{10}$........ cups

Write the total amount of juice as a mixed number. ....$1\frac{3}{10}$........ cups

3 Look at the denominators in **Model It**. What do you notice about the relationship between the original denominators, 2 and 5, and the common denominator, 10?

The common denominator is product of the original denominators, 2 and 5.

4 Is 10 the only common denominator for 2 and 5? Justify your answer.

No; Possible answers: All common multiples of 2 and 5 could be common denominators for 2 and 5, for example 10, 20 or 30 could be used as a common denominator.

5 Explain how to add two fractions with unlike denominators.

6 **REFLECT**

Look back at your **Try It**, strategies by classmates, and **Picture It** and **Model It**. Which models or strategies do you like best for adding fractions with unlike denominators? Explain.

....

....

....

....

Lesson 12 Add Fractions   **233**

APPLY IT

Use what you just learned to solve these problems.

7 Hank practices $\frac{5}{8}$ of the words on his spelling list on Monday. He practices another $\frac{1}{4}$ of his list on Tuesday. What fraction of his spelling list has Hank practiced so far? Show your work.

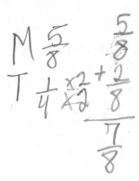

$$M\frac{5}{8} \qquad \frac{5}{8}$$
$$T\frac{1}{4}\times2 + \frac{2}{8}$$
$$\frac{7}{8}$$

Solution $\frac{7}{8}$

8 What is the sum of $\frac{7}{6}$ and $\frac{5}{8}$? Show your work.

$$\frac{7\times4}{6\times4} = \frac{28}{24}$$

$$39-24=15$$

$$\begin{array}{r}\frac{7}{6}\\+\frac{5}{8}\end{array}$$

$$\frac{5\times3}{8\times3} \quad \frac{15}{24} \quad \begin{array}{r}15\\+24\\\hline 39\end{array}$$

Solution $\frac{39}{24}$ or $1\frac{15}{24}$

9 What is the value of the expression $\frac{2}{3} + \frac{5}{12}$?

Ⓐ $\frac{7}{36}$

Ⓑ $\frac{7}{15}$

$$\frac{2\times4=8}{3\times4=12} + \frac{5}{12} = \frac{13}{12} \text{ or } 1\frac{1}{12}$$

Ⓒ $\frac{13}{12}$

Ⓓ $\frac{38}{36}$

©Curriculum Associates, LLC Copying is not permitted

Develop Adding with Mixed Numbers

Read and try to solve the problem below.

> Jenna spent $1\frac{2}{3}$ hours mowing the back yard. After taking a break, she spent $\frac{3}{4}$ hour mowing the front yard. How many hours did she spend mowing the whole yard?

TRY IT

 **Math Toolkit**
- fraction tiles
- fraction circles
- fractions bars
- grid paper
- number lines

DISCUSS IT

Ask your partner: Can you explain that again?

Tell your partner: I do not understand how . . .

Explore different ways to understand adding with mixed numbers.

Jenna spent $1\frac{2}{3}$ hours mowing the back yard. After taking a break, she spent $\frac{3}{4}$ hour mowing the front yard. How many hours did she spend mowing the whole yard?

PICTURE IT

You can picture the fractions in the problem using models.

The shaded parts represent time spent on the back yard, $1\frac{2}{3}$ hours, and the front yard, $\frac{3}{4}$ hour.

$1\frac{2}{3}$ hours $\quad+\quad$ $\frac{3}{4}$ hours

The sections need to be divided into same-size parts to add. Use dashed lines to divide the fraction models into 12 equal parts.

$1\frac{8}{12}$ hours $\quad+\quad$ $\frac{9}{12}$ hours $\qquad =\qquad$ $1\frac{17}{12}$

$2\frac{5}{12}$

MODEL IT

You can use a number line to add fractions.

The number line is divided first into thirds and then into twelfths, with a point at $1\frac{2}{3}$.

$\frac{1}{4} = \frac{3}{12}$, so $\frac{3}{4} = \frac{3}{12} + \frac{3}{12} + \frac{3}{12}$.

$\frac{3}{12} + \frac{3}{12} + \frac{3}{12} = \frac{9}{12}$

Start at $1\frac{2}{3}$ and jump right a total of $\frac{9}{12}$.

©Curriculum Associates, LLC   Copying is not permitted

CONNECT IT

Now you will use the problem from the previous page to help you understand how to add with mixed numbers.

1 Look at the models on the previous page. What is a common denominator of

$1\frac{2}{3}$ and $\frac{3}{4}$? ....

2 You can find this common denominator without a model. Write a multiplication equation that shows how the denominators 3 and 4 are related to 12.

....

3 Use this common denominator to find equivalent fractions for $1\frac{2}{3}$ and $\frac{3}{4}$.

$$1\frac{2}{3} + \frac{3}{4} = 1\frac{\square}{12} + \frac{\square}{12}$$

Then write the sum as a mixed number.

$$= 1\frac{\square}{12}$$

4 The fractional part of the mixed number in problem 3 is more than 1. How could you rewrite the mixed number so that its fractional part is less than 1?

How many hours did Jenna spend mowing the whole yard? ....

5 Explain how to add with mixed numbers.

6 REFLECT

Look back at your **Try It**, strategies by classmates, and **Picture It** and **Model It**. Which models or strategies do you like best for adding with mixed numbers? Explain.

....

....

....

APPLY IT

Use what you just learned to solve these problems.

7 What is the sum $1\frac{1}{6} + 2\frac{3}{8}$? Show your work.

$$1\frac{4}{24}$$
$$+2\frac{9}{24}$$
$$3\frac{13}{24}$$

Solution $3\frac{13}{24}$

8 Cameron has $4\frac{3}{4}$ pounds of raspberries, $2\frac{1}{8}$ pounds of blueberries, and $\frac{1}{2}$ pound of blackberries to make a fruit salad. How many pounds of fruit does Cameron have in all? Show your work.

$$R\ 4\frac{3}{4} = \frac{6}{8}$$
$$B\ 2\frac{1}{8} = \frac{1}{8}$$
$$+\frac{1}{2} = \frac{4}{8}$$
$$7\frac{3}{8} \qquad 6\frac{11}{8} \text{ or } 7\frac{3}{8}$$

Solution $7\frac{3}{8}$

9 What is the value of the expression $5\frac{3}{5} + 4\frac{1}{15}$? Show your work.

$$5 \quad \frac{3}{5} = \frac{9}{15}$$
$$+4 \quad \frac{1}{15} = \frac{1}{15}$$
$$9\frac{10}{15}$$

Solution $9\frac{10}{15}$

   ©Curriculum Associates, LLC   Copying is not permitted

Subtract Fractions

Dear Family,

This week your child is learning to subtract fractions with unlike denominators.

Your child might see a problem like this:

> Hailey needs $2\frac{1}{4}$ cups of almond milk for a recipe. She has $\frac{1}{2}$ cup. How much more almond milk does Hailey need?

One way to model subtracting $\frac{1}{2}$ from $2\frac{1}{4}$ is with a number line.

Start at the point $2\frac{1}{4}$.

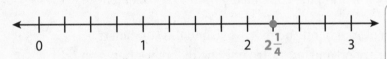

> Each whole on the number line is divided into 4 equal parts.

To subtract $\frac{1}{2}$, you need to find a common denominator with the fraction in $2\frac{1}{4}$.

The number 4 is a multiple of 2 and 4, so 4 is a common denominator.

Because $\frac{1}{2}$ is equivalent to $\frac{2}{4}$, you can start at $2\frac{1}{4}$ and jump back (left) $\frac{2}{4}$.

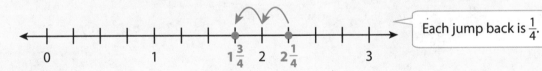

> Each jump back is $\frac{1}{4}$.

The number line shows that $2\frac{1}{4} - \frac{1}{2} = 1\frac{3}{4}$. Hailey needs $1\frac{3}{4}$ cups of almond milk.

Some other ways your child can think about subtracting fractions include using fraction bars or using multiplication to replace the given fractions with equivalent fractions that have the same denominator.

Invite your child to share what he or she knows about subtracting fractions by doing the following activity together.

©Curriculum Associates, LLC   Copying is not permitted

ACTIVITY SUBTRACTING FRACTIONS

Do this activity with your child to subtract fractions.

Materials ruler, yardstick, or measuring tape, and a variety of household objects

Work with your child to compare the lengths or heights of various objects around your home.

- Find two objects and measure their lengths. Measure the length of one object to the nearest $\frac{1}{2}$ inch and the length of the second object to the nearest $\frac{1}{8}$ or $\frac{1}{16}$ inch.

  Examples: lengths of fork and spoon, lengths of hand and foot

- Determine how much longer one object is than the other.

- Continue to practice adding fractions by finding the combined length of two or more objects and then comparing the combined length to another length.

- Find the combined length of your hand and foot. Next, find the combined length of a family member's hand and foot. Then find the difference between the two combined lengths.

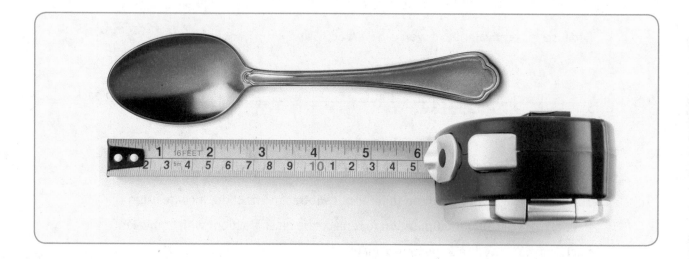

Look for other real-world examples of subtracting fractions with your child.

©Curriculum Associates, LLC   Copying is not permitted

Explore Subtracting Fractions

In the previous lesson, you learned about adding fractions. Now you will learn about subtracting fractions. Use what you know to try to solve the problem below.

Paul has a $\frac{3}{4}$-inch long bolt.
He buys a bolt that is $\frac{1}{8}$ inch longer
and a bolt that is $\frac{1}{8}$ inch shorter
than the $\frac{3}{4}$-inch bolt. What are the
lengths of the two bolts he buys?

Florida Standards

5.NF.1.1 Add and subtract fractions with unlike denominators (including mixed numbers) by replacing given fractions with equivalent fractions in such a way as to produce an equivalent sum or difference of fractions with like denominators.
5.NF.1.2

TRY IT

$$\frac{3}{4} \quad \frac{6}{8}$$

$$\frac{6}{8}$$
$$-\frac{1}{8}$$
shorter $\frac{5}{8}$

$$\frac{6}{8}$$
$$+\frac{1}{8}$$
longer $\frac{7}{8}$

🧰 **Math Toolkit**
- fraction tiles
- fraction circles
- fraction bars
- grid paper
- number lines

DISCUSS IT

Ask your partner: Can you explain that again?

Tell your partner: I started by . . .

©Curriculum Associates, LLC   Copying is not permitted

CONNECT IT

① LOOK BACK

Explain how to find the lengths of the two bolts Paul buys.

② LOOK AHEAD

Just like with adding fractions, you must find a common denominator to subtract fractions with unlike denominators, such as $\frac{3}{4} - \frac{1}{3}$.

a. Write the first four multiples of each denominator. Then circle the common multiple to find a common denominator.

Multiples of 4: ......4...... , ...8...... , ...12...... , ...16......

Multiples of 3: ......3...... , ...6...... , ...9...... , ...12......

b. Complete the missing numbers to write the equivalent fraction for $\frac{1}{3}$ using the common denominator of 12.

$$\frac{3 \times 3}{4 \times 3} = \frac{9}{12} \qquad \frac{1 \times \boxed{4}}{3 \times \boxed{4}} = \frac{\boxed{4}}{12}$$

c. The model below shows the equivalent fraction for $\frac{3}{4}$. Mark the model to subtract the fraction that is equivalent to $\frac{1}{3}$. Then use the equivalent fractions to write the subtraction equation shown by the model.

③ REFLECT

How is subtracting fractions like adding fractions?

....

....

....

©Curriculum Associates, LLC   Copying is not permitted

Develop Subtracting Fractions with Unlike Denominators

Read and try to solve the problem below.

> Gavin has $\frac{2}{3}$ pint of water left in his water bottle.
>
> He drinks $\frac{1}{2}$ pint. How much water is left in the bottle now?

TRY IT

 Math Toolkit
- fraction tiles
- fraction circles
- fraction bars
- grid paper
- number lines

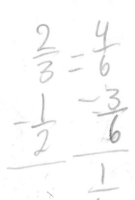

$$\frac{2}{3} = \frac{4}{6}$$
$$-\frac{1}{2} \quad -\frac{3}{6}$$
$$\frac{?}{?} \quad \frac{1}{6}$$

DISCUSS IT

Ask your partner: How did you get started?

Tell your partner: I am not sure how to find the answer because . . .

©Curriculum Associates, LLC   Copying is not permitted   **Lesson 13** Subtract Fractions   **253**

Explore different ways to understand subtracting fractions with unlike denominators.

Gavin has $\frac{2}{3}$ pint of water left in his water bottle. He drinks $\frac{1}{2}$ pint. How much water is left in the bottle now?

PICTURE IT

You can use a picture to model subtracting fractions.

The water bottle is marked to show that it has $\frac{2}{3}$ pint of water in it. Gavin drinks $\frac{1}{2}$ pint of water.

Use equivalent fractions to find a common denominator.

$$\frac{2}{3} = \frac{4}{6}$$

$$\frac{1}{2} = \frac{3}{6}$$

Now the water bottle is marked to show sixths. You can subtract $\frac{3}{6}$ from $\frac{4}{6}$.

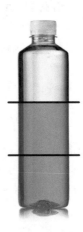

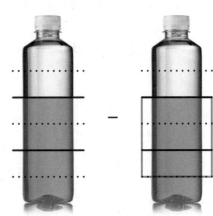

MODEL IT

You can use a number line to model subtracting fractions.

The number line below is divided into sixths, the common denominator.

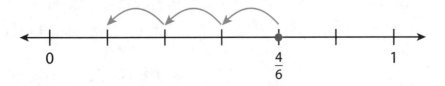

Start at $\frac{4}{6}$ and jump left $\frac{3}{6}$. $\left(\frac{3}{6}$ is three $\frac{1}{6}$ units on the number line.$\right)$

©Curriculum Associates, LLC Copying is not permitted

CONNECT IT
Now you will use the problem from the previous page to help you understand how to use equivalent fractions to subtract.

1 Look at **Picture It** and **Model It** from the previous page. Why is $\frac{2}{3}$ rewritten as $\frac{4}{6}$? Why is $\frac{1}{2}$ rewritten as $\frac{3}{6}$?

2 Why are sixths chosen as a common denominator?

3 Use sixths as a common denominator. Write an equation to show the difference of $\frac{2}{3}$ and $\frac{1}{2}$.

....

4 How much water is left in the bottle? ....

5 Could you have subtracted with a different common denominator? Provide an example.

6 Explain how to subtract two fractions with unlike denominators.

7 REFLECT

Look back at your **Try It**, strategies by classmates, and **Picture It** and **Model It**. Which models or strategies do you like best for subtracting fractions with unlike denominators? Explain.

....

....

....

APPLY IT

Use what you just learned to solve these problems.

8 What is $\frac{7}{8} - \frac{1}{6}$? Show your work.

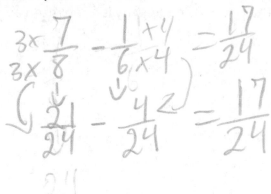

$$3 \times \frac{7}{8} - \frac{1 \times 4}{6 \times 4} = \frac{17}{24}$$

$$\left(\frac{21}{24} - \frac{4}{24} \right) = \frac{17}{24}$$

Solution $\underline{17/24}$

9 Emily's shelf is $\frac{3}{4}$ foot wide. Her clock is $\frac{2}{3}$ foot wide.

How much wider is her shelf than her clock? Show your work.

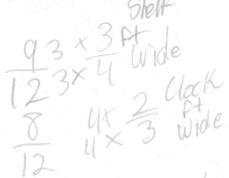

Shelf
$$\frac{9}{12} \quad \frac{3 \times 3}{3 \times 4} \quad \text{At wide}$$
$$- \frac{8}{12} \quad \frac{4 \times 2}{4 \times 3} \quad \text{Clock At wide}$$

Solution $\underline{1/12 \text{ wider}}$

10 What is the value of the expression $\frac{9}{10} - \frac{3}{5}$? Show your work.

$$\frac{1 \times 9}{1 \times 10} = \frac{9}{10}$$
$$- \frac{2 \times 3}{2 \times 5} = \frac{6}{10}$$
$$\frac{3}{10}$$

Solution $\underline{3/10}$

©Curriculum Associates, LLC   Copying is not permitted

Develop Subtracting with Mixed Numbers

Read and try to solve the problem below.

On Saturday, Chloe spent $3\frac{1}{4}$ hours at the park with her family. Then she spent $1\frac{2}{3}$ hours riding her bike. How much longer did Chloe spend at the park than riding her bike? Give your answer as a number of hours.

TRY IT

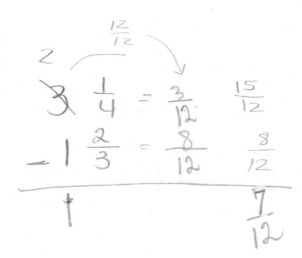

$$\begin{array}{r} \frac{12}{12} \\ 2 \\ \cancel{3}\ \frac{1}{4} = \frac{3}{12} \quad \frac{15}{12} \\ -1\ \frac{2}{3} = \frac{8}{12} \quad \frac{8}{12} \\ \hline 1 \qquad \frac{7}{12} \end{array}$$

 **Math Toolkit**

- fraction tiles
- fraction circles
- fraction bars
- grid paper
- number lines

DISCUSS IT

Ask your partner: Why did you choose that strategy?

Tell your partner: A model I used was . . . It helped me . . .

©Curriculum Associates, LLC   Copying is not permitted

Explore different ways to understand subtracting with mixed numbers.

On Saturday, Chloe spent $3\frac{1}{4}$ hours at the park with her family. Then she spent $1\frac{2}{3}$ hours riding her bike. How much longer did Chloe spend at the park than riding her bike? Give your answer as a number of hours.

PICTURE IT

You can use fraction bars to picture subtracting with mixed numbers.

Chloe spent $3\frac{1}{4}$ hours at the park. To subtract $1\frac{2}{3}$ hours, find a common denominator.

Hours spent at the park: $3\frac{1}{4} = 3\frac{3}{12}$ Hours spent riding her bike: $1\frac{2}{3} = 1\frac{8}{12}$

Model $3\frac{3}{12}$.

You need **more twelfths** to subtract $1\frac{8}{12}$.

$3\frac{3}{12} = 2\frac{15}{12}$

MODEL IT

You can use equations to subtract mixed numbers.

You can regroup one whole and break apart the mixed numbers to find $3\frac{3}{12} - 1\frac{8}{12}$.

3 wholes and $\frac{3}{12}$ is the same as 2 wholes and $\frac{15}{12}$.

$2 - 1 = 1$ and $\frac{15}{12} - \frac{8}{12} = \frac{7}{12}$

©Curriculum Associates, LLC   Copying is not permitted

CONNECT IT

Now you will use the problem from the previous page to help you understand how to subtract mixed numbers with regrouping.

1 Look at the first set of fraction bars in **Picture It**. Why is the last bar split into 12 pieces instead of 4 pieces?

2 Now look at the second set of fraction bars in **Picture It**. Explain why $3\frac{3}{12}$ is now shown as $2\frac{15}{12}$.

3 Look at **Model It**. How does the regrouping of $3\frac{3}{12}$ as $2\frac{15}{12}$ help you find how much longer Chloe spent at the park than riding her bike?

4 How much longer did Chloe spend at the park than riding her bike? .... hour(s)

5 Show how you can use addition to check your answer.

6 Do you always need to regroup when you subtract mixed numbers with unlike denominators? Explain.

7 REFLECT

Look back at your **Try It**, strategies by classmates, and **Picture It** and **Model It**. Which models or strategies do you like best for subtracting mixed numbers? Explain.

....

....

....

APPLY IT

Use what you just learned to solve these problems.

8 What is $7\frac{3}{5} - \frac{9}{10}$? Show your work.

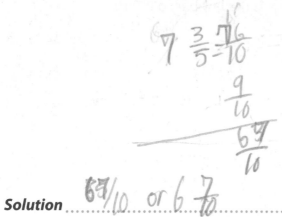

$$7 \frac{3}{5} = \frac{76}{10}$$

$$\frac{9}{10}$$

$$\frac{67}{10}$$

Solution $\frac{67}{10}$ or $6\frac{7}{10}$

9 What is the difference between $2\frac{5}{8}$ and $1\frac{1}{4}$? Show your work.

$$2\frac{5}{8}$$
$$-1\frac{1}{4} \quad \frac{2}{8}$$
$$1\frac{3}{8}$$

Solution $1\frac{3}{8}$

10 Charlie is practicing the long jump. His first jump is a distance of $16\frac{5}{6}$ feet. His second jump is a distance of $18\frac{2}{3}$ feet. How much longer is Charlie's second jump?

Ⓐ $1\frac{1}{6}$ feet

Ⓑ $1\frac{5}{6}$ feet

Ⓒ $2\frac{1}{6}$ feet

Ⓓ $2\frac{5}{6}$ feet

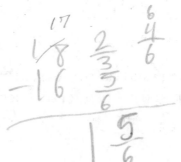

$$\cancel{18} \quad \frac{2}{3} \quad \frac{4}{6}$$
$$-16 \quad \frac{5}{6}$$
$$1\frac{5}{6}$$

Add and Subtract in Word Problems

Dear Family,

This week your child is learning to add and subtract fractions and decimals in word problems.

Your child is also learning to estimate the answer in order to check whether an answer is reasonable or not. He or she might see a problem like this:

> *Paul used $\frac{5}{8}$ cup of milk to make muffins and $\frac{1}{3}$ cup of milk to make nut bread. How much milk did Paul use to make muffins and nut bread?*

To solve the problem, add the fractions $\frac{5}{8}$ and $\frac{1}{3}$.

It can be helpful to show the fractions on number lines.

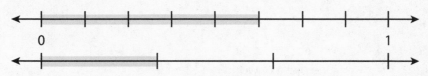

To estimate the sum, you can use a benchmark fraction for each fraction in the problem. Here, $\frac{1}{2}$ is a good benchmark fraction to use.

$\frac{5}{8}$ is close to $\frac{1}{2}$ and $\frac{1}{3}$ is close to $\frac{1}{2}$. Since $\frac{1}{2} + \frac{1}{2} = 1$, an estimate of $\frac{5}{8} + \frac{1}{3}$ is about 1.

Now add the fractions $\frac{5}{8} + \frac{1}{3}$. The fractions need to have equal-size parts, so write equivalent fractions with like denominators. Then add.

$$\frac{5}{8} = \frac{15}{24} \qquad \frac{1}{3} = \frac{8}{24}$$
$$\frac{15}{24} + \frac{8}{24} = \frac{23}{24}$$

Is a sum of $\frac{23}{24}$ a reasonable answer? Check the sum against the estimate you made. The estimate is about 1, and $\frac{23}{24}$ is about 1, so the sum is reasonable.

Invite your child to share what he or she knows about adding and subtracting fractions in word problems by doing the following activity together.

ACTIVITY ADDING AND SUBTRACTING FRACTIONS IN WORD PROBLEMS

Do this activity with your child to add and subtract in word problems.

Work together with your child to identify some real-world situations when you might use fractions, such as when you are cooking, building, or gardening.

- Here are some examples in which you might add and subtract fractions:

A recipe for soup calls for $2\frac{1}{3}$ cups of water and $1\frac{3}{8}$ cups of milk.

One piece of wood is $4\frac{1}{2}$ feet long and another piece is $2\frac{2}{3}$ feet long.

A string used for tomato plants is $3\frac{3}{4}$ feet long. Another string is $2\frac{1}{3}$ feet long.

Choose one of the examples above. Add the mixed numbers in that example. Work together to first make an estimate of the sum. Check your answer against the estimate to make sure your answer is reasonable.

©Curriculum Associates, LLC Copying is not permitted

Explore Adding and Subtracting in Word Problems

Now that you can add and subtract fractions with different denominators, you can use this skill to solve word problems. Use what you know to try to solve the problem below.

> Aleena has a 1-gallon watering can that is full of water. She uses $\frac{3}{8}$ gallon to water her roses and $\frac{1}{3}$ gallon to water her geraniums. How much water did Aleena use to water both the roses and geraniums?

Florida Standards

5.NF.1.2 Solve word problems involving addition and subtraction of fractions referring to the same whole, including cases of unlike denominators, e.g., by using visual fraction models or equations to represent the problem. Use benchmark fractions and number sense of fractions to estimate mentally and assess the reasonableness of answers.

5.NBT.1.4, 5.NBT.2.7, 5.NF.1.1

TRY IT

🧰 Math Toolkit
- fraction tiles
- fraction circles
- fraction bars
- grid paper
- number lines

DISCUSS IT

Ask your partner: How did you get started?

Tell your partner: I knew . . . so I . . .

CONNECT IT

1 **LOOK BACK**

Explain how you found how much water Aleena used to water both the roses and the geraniums.

2 **LOOK AHEAD**

A benchmark fraction is a common fraction that you can easily compare to other fractions. The number line below shows the location of some benchmark fractions between 0 and 2. You can use these fractions to estimate sums and differences.

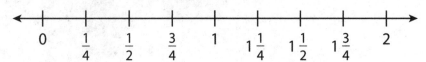

a. Between which two benchmark fractions is $\frac{3}{8}$? How do you know?

b. Between which two benchmark fractions is $\frac{1}{3}$? How do you know?

c. Use your answers from parts a and b above to find a low estimate for the sum $\frac{3}{8} + \frac{1}{3}$ and a high estimate for the sum $\frac{3}{8} + \frac{1}{3}$. Explain your reasoning.

3 **REFLECT**

The actual sum of any two fractions will be somewhere between a low estimate and a high estimate for the sum. How does the actual sum you found in problem 1 compare to your low estimate and high estimate for the sum?

©Curriculum Associates, LLC Copying is not permitted

Prepare for Adding and Subtracting in Word Problems

1 Think about what you know about benchmark fractions. Fill in each box. Use words, numbers, and pictures. Show as many ideas as you can.

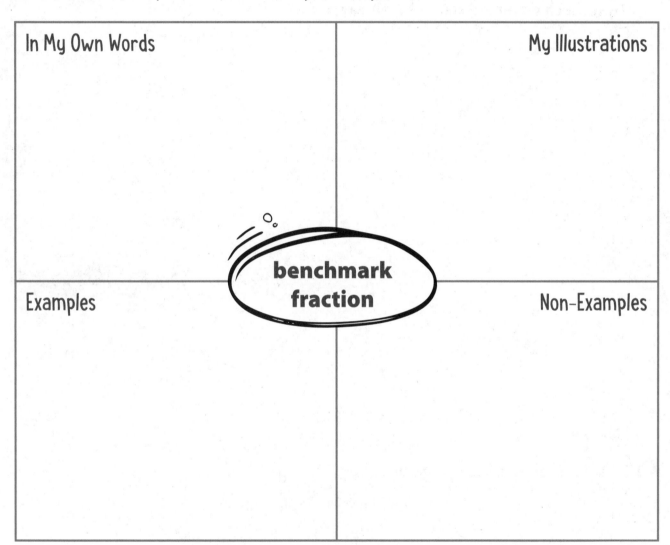

In My Own Words

My Illustrations

Examples

benchmark fraction

Non-Examples

2 Between which two benchmark fractions is $\frac{5}{8}$? How do you know?

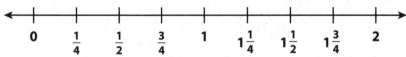

0   $\frac{1}{4}$ $\frac{1}{2}$ $\frac{3}{4}$ 1 $1\frac{1}{4}$ $1\frac{1}{2}$ $1\frac{3}{4}$ 2

©Curriculum Associates, LLC   Copying is not permitted

3 Solve the problem. Show your work.

Hai has a 1-gallon jug of water. He drinks $\frac{1}{8}$ gallon of water before lunch and $\frac{2}{3}$ gallon of water after lunch. How much water did Hai drink all day?

Solution ....

4 Check your answer. Show your work.

   ©Curriculum Associates, LLC   Copying is not permitted

Develop Estimating in Word Problems with Fractions

Read and try to solve the problem below.

> Frankie purchases a $3\frac{1}{2}$-pound bag of chicken.
> He uses $1\frac{1}{3}$ pounds of chicken for fajitas.
> How many pounds of chicken does Frankie
> have left? Estimate and solve. Tell if your
> answer is reasonable.

TRY IT

 **Math Toolkit**
- fraction tiles
- fraction circles
- fraction bars
- grid paper
- number lines

DISCUSS IT

Ask your partner: Do you agree with me? Why or why not?

Tell your partner: I disagree with this part because . . .

©Curriculum Associates, LLC   Copying is not permitted

Explore different ways to understand estimating with fractions.

Frankie purchases a $3\frac{1}{2}$-pound bag of chicken.
He uses $1\frac{1}{3}$ pounds of chicken for fajitas. How many
pounds of chicken does Frankie have left?
Estimate and solve. Tell if your answer is reasonable.

MODEL IT

You can use a number line to find benchmark fractions to estimate.

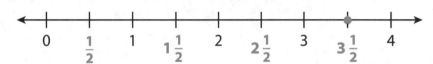

$3\frac{1}{2}$ is already a benchmark fraction you can use to estimate.

You can find a benchmark fraction close to $1\frac{1}{3}$ to help you estimate the difference.

MODEL IT

You can model the problem with a number line.

Since $2 \times 3 = 6$, the fractions in the problem, $3\frac{1}{2}$ and $1\frac{1}{3}$, can be rewritten using a common denominator of 6. $3\frac{1}{2} = 3\frac{3}{6}$, and $1\frac{1}{3} = 1\frac{2}{6}$.

The number line below is divided into sixths. It shows starting with a total of $3\frac{1}{2}$ pounds and then making two jumps to the left for the $1\frac{1}{3}$ pounds of chicken used.

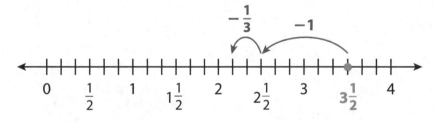

You can rewrite $3\frac{1}{2} - 1\frac{1}{3}$ as $3\frac{3}{6} - 1\frac{2}{6}$.

 ©Curriculum Associates, LLC Copying is not permitted

CONNECT IT

Now you will use the problem from the previous page to help you understand how to use estimation with adding and subtracting fractions.

1 Look at the first **Model It**. Identify the closest half on each side of $1\frac{1}{3}$.

$1\frac{1}{3}$ is greater than .... and less than ....

Why are halves a good choice for benchmark fractions for $1\frac{1}{3}$?

2 Use one of the benchmark fractions for $1\frac{1}{3}$ that you found in problem 1 to estimate how many pounds of chicken Frankie has left. Write a subtraction equation to show your estimated difference.

3 Use the common denominator found in the second **Model It** to find the actual difference. How many pounds of chicken does Frankie have left?

4 Is the actual difference greater than or less than your estimate in problem 2? Why?

5 Explain how you can check if a fraction sum or difference is reasonable.

6 REFLECT

Look back at your **Try It**, strategies by classmates, and **Model Its**. Which models or strategies do you like best for estimating with fractions? Explain.

....

....

....

Lesson 14 Add and Subtract in Word Problems   **277**

APPLY IT

Use what you just learned to solve these problems.

7 Tim's bean sprout grew $3\frac{3}{8}$ inches. Teegan's bean sprout grew $2\frac{3}{4}$ inches. How many more inches did Tim's bean sprout grow than Teegan's?

Estimate to tell if your solution is reasonable. Show your work.

Tim's bean sprout grew .... more than Teegan's bean sprout.

8 Samantha likes to run at least 5 miles each day. She plans a new course: from home to the park is $1\frac{1}{3}$ miles, from the park to the library is $2\frac{2}{5}$ miles, and from the park to home is $\frac{2}{3}$ mile. Will Samantha run at least 5 miles on this new course?

Use only estimation to decide. Then explain if you are confident in your estimate or if you need to find an actual sum. Show your work.

Samantha .... run at least 5 miles.

©Curriculum Associates, LLC   Copying is not permitted

Practice Estimating in Word Problems with Fractions

Study the Example showing how to estimate a sum using benchmark fractions. Then solve problems 1–5.

EXAMPLE

David grew $1\frac{3}{4}$ inches last year and $1\frac{5}{8}$ inches this year. Estimate how much he grew in the two years.

You can estimate $1\frac{3}{4} + 1\frac{5}{8}$ using benchmark fractions. The number line below shows common fractions used as benchmark fractions to estimate sums and differences.

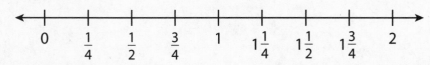

$1\frac{3}{4}$ is one of the benchmark fractions. $1\frac{5}{8}$ is a little greater than $1\frac{1}{2}$. Estimate using $1\frac{1}{2}$.

$$1\frac{3}{4} + 1\frac{1}{2} = 1\frac{3}{4} + 1\frac{2}{4} = 2\frac{5}{4}, \text{ or } 3\frac{1}{4}.$$

The sum is a little greater than $3\frac{1}{4}$, so David grew a little more than $3\frac{1}{4}$ inches.

1 Look at the Example. Shade the fraction bars below to show that $1\frac{5}{8}$ is a little greater than $1\frac{1}{2}$.

$1\frac{5}{8}$ [   ] [   ]

$1\frac{1}{2}$ [   ] [   ]

2 Find the actual sum $1\frac{3}{4} + 1\frac{5}{8}$ to determine how much David grew in two years. Use the estimate to explain how you know your answer is reasonable. Show your work.

Solution ....

....

Irene makes $4\frac{2}{3}$ cups of pancake batter. She splits the batter into 2 bowls. She mixes blueberries into $2\frac{1}{4}$ cups of batter and walnuts into the rest of the batter.

3 Estimate how much of the batter has walnuts in it. Explain your estimate.

4 Find the actual amount of batter that has walnuts in it.
Explain how you know your answer is reasonable. Show your work.

Solution

5 Irene makes a second batch of $3\frac{1}{4}$ cups of pancake batter. She wants to know how much more batter she made in the first batch. She estimates that the difference between the sizes of the two batches is $2\frac{1}{12}$. Explain why this estimate is *not* reasonable.

 ©Curriculum Associates, LLC   Copying is not permitted

Develop Using Estimation with Decimals

Read and try to solve the problem below.

> Scott is conducting a science experiment. He has
> 3.74 liters of Liquid A and 3.65 liters of Liquid B.
> He pours both liquids into a container.
>
> How much liquid is in the container?
> Estimate and solve. Tell if your answer is reasonable.

TRY IT

Math Toolkit

- base-ten blocks
- base-ten grid paper
- decimal grids
- number lines
- place-value charts

DISCUSS IT

Ask your partner: Can you explain that again?

Tell your partner: I agree with you about . . . because . . .

©Curriculum Associates, LLC   Copying is not permitted

Explore different ways to understand estimating with decimals.

> **Scott is conducting a science experiment. He has 3.74 liters of Liquid A and 3.65 liters of Liquid B. He pours both liquids into a container.**
>
> **How much liquid is in the container? Estimate and solve. Tell if your answer is reasonable.**

PICTURE IT

You can picture an estimate of the problem using decimal grids.

Both 3.74 liters and 3.65 liters are about 4 liters.

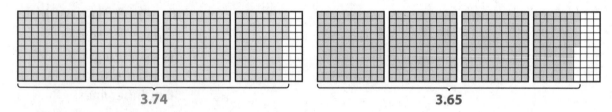

An estimate of the sum is 4 + 4.

The actual sum can be found by finding 3.74 + 3.65.

MODEL IT

You can use a number line to help estimate.

3.74 and 3.65 are both between 3.5 and 4.

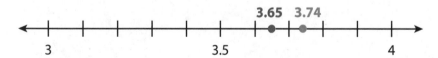

An estimate of the sum is 3.5 + 3.5.

The actual sum can be found by finding 3.74 + 3.65.

   ©Curriculum Associates, LLC   Copying is not permitted

CONNECT IT

Now you will use the problem from the previous page to help you understand how to estimate with decimals.

1 Look at **Picture It**. Why is 4 a good number to use for each addend in an estimated sum?

2 Is the actual sum of the measures of Liquids A and B in **Picture It** less than or greater than the estimated sum? Why?

3 Look at **Model It**. Why is 3.5 a good number to use for each addend in an estimated sum?

4 Is the actual sum of the measures of Liquids A and B in **Model It** less than or greater than the estimated sum? Why?

5 Explain how you can check if a decimal sum or difference is reasonable.

6 REFLECT

Look back at your **Try It**, strategies by classmates, and **Picture It** and **Model It**. Which models or strategies do you like best for estimating with decimals? Explain.

....

....

APPLY IT

Use what you just learned to solve these problems.

7 Sean has 12.6 meters of garden netting. He needs 15.85 meters to enclose his garden. How many more meters of netting does Sean need to buy? Estimate to tell if your solution is reasonable. Show your work.

Sean needs .... meters more of garden netting.

8 Erika wants at least 6 pounds of apples for a recipe. She picks a 2.56-pound bag of red apples, a 1.18-pound bag of green apples, and a 2.79-pound bag of yellow apples. Does Erika need to pick more apples?

Use estimation only to decide. Then explain if you are confident in your estimate or if you need to find an actual sum. Show your work.

Erika .... to pick more apples.

9 Vinh is having lunch at a café. He has $15 in his pocket and has already ordered a sandwich for $8.57 and a drink for $2.34. Vinh also wants to buy a side salad for $5.25. Does he have enough money? Estimate or find an exact answer to solve. Show your work.

Vinh .... enough money.

©Curriculum Associates, LLC   Copying is not permitted

Practice Using Estimation with Decimals

**Study the Example showing how to estimate a difference using decimal grids.
Then solve problems 1–4.**

EXAMPLE

Kamala has 2.73 liters of lemonade. She wants to have about 5.5 liters for her party. About how much more lemonade does Kamala need?

One way to estimate is to round to the nearest tenth.
5.5 is given to the nearest tenth. **2.73** is about **2.7**.

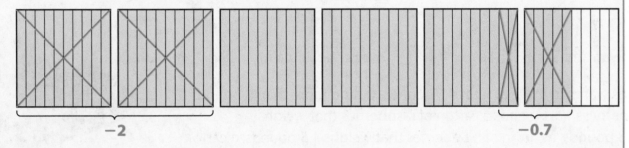

−2   −0.7

Kamala needs about 2.8 liters more of lemonade.

1   Look at the Example. Does this situation require an exact answer, or is the estimate enough? Explain.

2   Suppose Kamala wants to have exactly 5.5 liters of lemonade for her party. How much more lemonade does she need? Show your work.

Kamala needs .... liters more of lemonade.

Lesson 14 Add and Subtract in Word Problems   **285**

3 Ryan and Sarah are looking at cell phone plans. They could share a group plan that costs $119.95 per month, or they could each pay for an individual plan that costs $62.77 per month.

a. Estimate which choice would cost less for Ryan and Sarah. Explain why.

b. How much money could they save per month by paying for the choice that costs less instead of the choice that costs more? Show your work.

Ryan and Sarah can save .... by choosing a(n) .... plan.

4 Chris wants to make at least 4.5 pounds, but no more than 5 pounds, of berry salad. He finds a carton of raspberries that weighs 1.83 pounds, a carton of blueberries that weighs 1.5 pounds, a carton of blackberries that weighs 1.72 pounds, and a carton of strawberries that weighs 1.29 pounds. If Chris wants to use three different types of berries, what is one combination of cartons he could buy? Explain. Show your work.

Solution ....

....

....

....

....

  ©Curriculum Associates, LLC Copying is not permitted

Refine Adding and Subtracting in Word Problems

Complete the Example below. Then solve problems 1–7.

EXAMPLE

Steven buys a movie ticket for $14.75 and then buys some snacks for the movie. He spends a total of $19.23. About how much did Steven spend on snacks?

Look at how you could show your work using a number line.

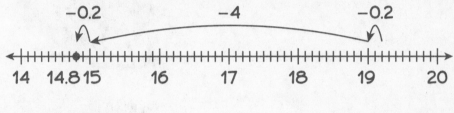

Solution ....

The student rounded to the nearest tenth to estimate the answer.

PAIR/SHARE
How do you know if the amount spent on snacks will be more or less than $4?

APPLY IT

1 Parker mixes $3\frac{1}{2}$ ounces of blue paint with $1\frac{2}{5}$ ounces of yellow paint to make green paint for the leaves of a tree. How many ounces of green paint did Parker make?

Estimate and then compute. Explain how you know your result is reasonable. Show your work.

Will there be a little more than $4\frac{1}{2}$ ounces or a little less than $4\frac{1}{2}$ ounces of green paint?

PAIR/SHARE
Was your estimate more than or less than the actual answer? By how much?

Solution ....

....

2 Jaime's football weighs 0.875 pound. His football helmet weighs 5.67 pounds. Estimate how much more the helmet weighs than the football. Explain your estimate. Show your work.

I could think about rounding to the nearest quarter, half, or whole pound, instead of to the nearest tenth or hundredth.

PAIR/SHARE
How does the exact difference compare to your estimate?

Solution ....

3 Which is a reasonable estimate for the difference $5\frac{1}{2} - 3\frac{5}{9}$?

Ⓐ between $\frac{1}{2}$ and 1

Ⓑ between 1 and $1\frac{1}{2}$

Ⓒ between $1\frac{1}{2}$ and 2

Ⓓ between 2 and $2\frac{1}{2}$

Elise chose Ⓓ as the correct answer. How did she get that answer?

How can you use benchmark fractions to estimate the difference?

PAIR/SHARE
Does Elise's answer make sense?

©Curriculum Associates, LLC   Copying is not permitted

4 William compares monthly rainfall amounts for the summer months using the table below.

Month	Monthly Rainfall
June	$3\frac{3}{10}$ inches
July	$3\frac{3}{4}$ inches
August	$3\frac{1}{2}$ inches

Which estimate is closest to the actual difference between the rainfall amounts for June and July?

Ⓐ $\frac{1}{4}$ inch

Ⓑ $\frac{1}{2}$ inch

Ⓒ 1 inch

Ⓓ $1\frac{1}{2}$ inches

5 Carter is at the school store. He wants to buy a pack of notebooks that costs $4.79, a calculator that costs $33.54, and a tablet case that costs $12.67. About how much money does Carter plan to spend at the school store? Will the actual cost be more or less than your estimate? Explain. Show your work.

Solution ....

....

6 A certain liquid boils at 175.62°F. The liquid is currently at 68.8°F. Jimmy says that the temperature needs to rise by about 125°F to boil.

Part A Without finding the actual difference, explain why Jimmy's estimate is or is not reasonable.

Part B Find the actual amount the temperature must rise for the liquid to boil. Show your work.

Solution ....

7 MATH JOURNAL

Ramona has $4\frac{1}{5}$ gallons of red paint. She knows she needs at least $12\frac{3}{4}$ gallons to paint her whole house. Use benchmark fractions to explain about how much more paint Ramona needs.

☑ SELF CHECK Go back to the Unit 2 Opener and see what you can check off.

Self Reflection

In this unit you learned to . . .

Skill	Lesson
Recognize that a digit in one place represents 10 times as much as it represents in the place to its right and $\frac{1}{10}$ of what it represents in the place to its left.	6
Use patterns to understand multiplying and dividing whole numbers and decimals.	7
Read and write decimals in different forms, for example: $80.63 = 8 \times 10 + 6 \times \frac{1}{10} + 3 \times \frac{1}{100}$.	8
Compare decimals, for example: $3.47 > 3.096$.	9
Round decimals, for example: 6.274 rounded to the nearest tenth is 6.3.	9
Add and subtract decimals, for example: $20.08 + 5.15 = 25.23$.	10, 11
Add and subtract fractions with unlike denominators, for example: $\frac{3}{5} + \frac{1}{4} = \frac{17}{20}$.	12, 13
Estimate sums and differences of fractions or decimals.	14

Think about what you have learned.

Use words, numbers, and drawings.

1 Three examples of what I learned are . . .

2 The hardest thing I learned to do is .... because . . .

3 I could use more practice with . . .

©Curriculum Associates, LLC   Copying is not permitted

Use Decimals and Fractions

Study an Example Problem and Solution

SMP 1 Make sense of problems and persevere in solving them.

Read this problem involving decimals. Then look at Alex's solution to this problem.

Dog Collars

Alex is organizing a pet fair. Money from the fair will be donated to the local pet shelter. Alex's friend Bella will have a booth at the fair. Here is Bella's sign.

Adorable Dog Collars	
Small	$10.75
Medium	$12.00
Large	$13.25

Supplies to make a small collar cost $1.60. Bella estimates that the supplies for each size collar cost $0.40 more than the next smaller size. Bella hopes to make at least $225 for the pet shelter by selling collars.

• Find how much Bella makes on each collar after paying for supplies.

• Show a way to make at least $225 by selling collars.

• Include at least 5 collars of each size in your plan.

Read the sample solution on the next page. Then look at the checklist below. Find and mark parts of the solution that match the checklist.

✓ PROBLEM-SOLVING CHECKLIST

☐ Tell what is known.

☐ Tell what the problem is asking.

☐ Show all your work.

☐ Show that the solution works.

a. **Circle** something that is known.

b. **Underline** something that you need to find.

c. **Draw a box around** what you do to solve the problem.

d. **Put a checkmark** next to the part that shows the solution works.

©Curriculum Associates, LLC   Copying is not permitted

ALEX'S SOLUTION

Hi, I'm Alex. Here's how I solved this problem.

- **I know the selling price** of each collar. **I need to find the cost to** make each size collar and subtract it from the price.

Size	Price	Cost of Supplies	Donation Amount
Small	$10.75	$1.60	$9.15
Medium	$12.00	$1.60 + $0.40 = $2.00	$10.00
Large	$13.25	$2.00 + $0.40 = $2.40	$10.85

I used a table to organize my information.

- **I'll round the donation amounts so that I can estimate.** I can multiply each rounded amount by 5 since I have to include at least 5 of each size collar.

$9.15 ⟶ $9   and $9 × 5 = $45

$10.00 ⟶ $10   and $10 × 5 = $50

$10.85 ⟶ $11   and $11 × 5 = $55

$45 + $50 + $55 = $150

By rounding and estimating first, I avoid some computing with decimals.

- **I can see** that I need about $75 more to get to $225. I can try to make about $25 with each of the three collar sizes.

$9 × 3 = $27 $10 × 3 = $30 $11 × 3 = $33

- **Now I can find the actual amounts from 5 + 3 small collars, 5 + 3 medium collars, and 5 + 3 large collars.**

- Since I want to sell 8 of each size collar, I can add together the donation amount from 1 of each size, then multiply by 8.

$9.15 + $10.00 + $10.85 = $30.00
$30 × 8 = $240

If Bella sells 8 of each size collar, she will be able to donate $240.

This is my final answer.

The solution works because it includes at least 5 collars of each size and it makes more than $225 for the shelter.

Try Another Approach

There are many ways to solve problems. Think about how you might solve the Dog Collars problem in a different way.

Dog Collars

Alex is organizing a pet fair. Money from the fair will be donated to the local pet shelter. Alex's friend Bella will have a booth at the fair. Here is Bella's sign.

> ### Adorable Dog Collars
>
> Small.. $10.75
>
> Medium....................................... $12.00
>
> Large $13.25

Supplies to make a small collar cost $1.60. Bella estimates that the supplies for each size collar cost $0.40 more than the next smaller size. Bella hopes to make at least $225 for the pet shelter by selling collars.

- Find how much Bella makes on each collar after paying for supplies.

- Show a way to make at least $225 by selling collars.

- Include at least 5 collars of each size in your plan.

PLAN IT

Answer these questions to help you start thinking about a plan.

A. How can you use estimation to help find a solution?

B. How can you use Alex's solution to plan how to find a different solution?

©Curriculum Associates, LLC   Copying is not permitted

SOLVE IT

Find a different solution for the Dog Collars problem. Show all your work on a separate sheet of paper.

You may want to use the Problem-Solving Tips to get started.

PROBLEM-SOLVING TIPS

- **Models** You might want to use . . .
  - number lines.
  - tables.

- **Word Bank**

round	multiply	greater than
estimate	product	decimal

- **Sentence Starters**
  - I can round _____
  - If I multiply _____

☑ **PROBLEM-SOLVING CHECKLIST**

Make sure that you . . .
- ☐ tell what you know.
- ☐ tell what you need to do.
- ☐ show all your work.
- ☐ show that the solution works.

REFLECT

Use Mathematical Practices As you work through the problem, discuss these questions with a partner.

- **Use Models** How can you use division to help find a solution?

- **Reason Mathematically** What strategies can you use to solve this problem?

Unit 2 Math in Action Use Decimals and Fractions   **295**

Discuss Models and Strategies

Read the problem. Write a solution on a separate sheet of paper. Remember, there can be lots of ways to solve a problem!

Petting Zoo

The zoo where Alex works has agreed to bring some animals to the pet fair. Guests can pay to feed and play with the animals. Alex has to decide which animals to bring and how much food they will need.

Petting Zoo Notes

- Include 2 or 3 different kinds of animals.
- Include more than 6 but fewer than 9 animals.
- Have enough food to feed each animal a day's worth of food.

Alex reads the keeper's notes to find about how much an average animal eats in a day.

How much food should Alex bring to the pet fair?

Keeper's Notes About Feeding Animals

Rabbit: $\frac{1}{8}$ pound of pellets and $\frac{1}{4}$ pound of vegetables.

Goat: $4\frac{1}{2}$ pounds of hay and $2\frac{1}{4}$ pounds of grains.

Small Pig: $5\frac{1}{2}$ pounds of food (mix of grains and vegetables, at least one pound of each food).

Calf: 10 pounds of hay and $4\frac{1}{2}$ pounds of grains

©Curriculum Associates, LLC   Copying is not permitted

PLAN IT AND SOLVE IT

Find a solution to the Petting Zoo problem.

Write a detailed plan for Alex. Be sure to include:

- which animals and how many of each to bring to the pet fair.

- a list of the food she will need to feed all the animals for one day, including amounts of each kind of food.

- reasons for the choices you made.

You may want to use the Problem-Solving Tips to get started.

PROBLEM-SOLVING TIPS

- **Questions**

  - How does the size of the animal affect your choice?

  - Which animals eat some of the same kind of food?

- **Sentence Starters**

  - I would bring _____

  - Alex needs about _____

☑ **PROBLEM-SOLVING CHECKLIST**

Make sure that you . . .
- ☐ tell what you know.
- ☐ tell what you need to do.
- ☐ show all your work.
- ☐ show that the solution works.

REFLECT

Use Mathematical Practices As you work through the problem, discuss these questions with a partner.

- **Make Sense of Problems** What will you do first? Why?

- **Make an Argument** How can you justify the choices you made?

Unit 2 Math in Action Use Decimals and Fractions   **297**

Persevere On Your Own

Read the problems. Write a solution on a separate sheet of paper.

Barely Used

Alex's friend Brandi has a collection of used books, CDs, and DVDs that people have given her. She will sell them at a booth at the pet fair. Brandi thinks she can sell enough items to make more than $100 donation to the pet shelter. Look at Brandi's prices.

- Paperback Books $0.95
- Hardcover Books $3.37
- DVDs $3.25
- CDs $1.95

What items can Brandi sell to make more than $100?

SOLVE IT

Find a combination of items that Brandi needs to sell to meet her goal.

- Include some of all four items.
- For each item, tell how many Brandi needs to sell and how much money she will make.
- Give the total amount Brandi will make selling all the items on your list.
- Explain why this total works.

REFLECT

Use Mathematical Practices After you complete the task, choose one of these questions to discuss with a partner.

- **Use Models** What equations or expressions did you use to find your solution?

- **Persevere** What were all of the steps you took to find a solution?

   ©Curriculum Associates, LLC   Copying is not permitted

Ring Toss

In a ring toss game, a player throws rings until four rings land around pegs. To find the score, add blue fractions (top row of pegs) and then subtract red fractions (bottom two rows). To win, the player's score must be at least 1, but no more than $1\frac{1}{4}$.

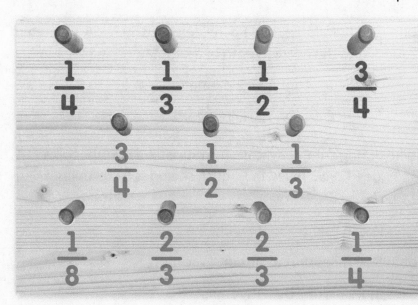

A player's first ring lands around the blue $\frac{3}{4}$ peg in the top row.
Where can the other three rings land so the player wins?

SOLVE IT

Tell a combination of three pegs that will let the player win.

• Tell which three pegs the rings could land on.

• Explain your choices.

• Show why your solution works.

REFLECT

Use Mathematical Practices After you complete the task, choose one of these questions to discuss with a partner.

• **Persevere** What are some different ways you could start your solution?

• **Make an Argument** How do you know the numbers you choose work?

1 Which number is equivalent to 0.15×10^3?

Ⓐ 0.015

Ⓑ 0.15

Ⓒ 15

Ⓓ 150

2 The driving distance between Buffalo, NY, and Rochester, NY, is 117.456 kilometers. What is this distance rounded to the nearest tenth of a kilometer?

Ⓐ 117 kilometers

Ⓑ 117.5 kilometers

Ⓒ 117.46 kilometers

Ⓓ 120 kilometers

3 Julie likes to ride her bike during summer vacation. In June, she rides her bike 104.78 miles. In July, she rides 129.53 miles. In August, she rides 61.05 miles. Which statements are true?

Ⓐ Julie rides 68.48 miles less in August than in July.

Ⓑ Julie rides a total of 295.36 miles during summer vacation.

Ⓒ Julie rides 43.73 miles more in June than in August.

Ⓓ Julie rides more miles in June than in July.

Ⓔ Rounded to the nearest tenth, Julie rides 129.6 miles in July.

4 Tell if each equation is *True* or *False*.

	True	False
$3\frac{4}{5} + 6\frac{2}{10} = 10$	Ⓐ	Ⓑ
$22\frac{7}{9} - 16\frac{1}{4} = 6\frac{19}{36}$	Ⓒ	Ⓓ
$\frac{2}{3} - \frac{1}{6} = \frac{1}{3}$	Ⓔ	Ⓕ
$6 + \frac{1}{5} = \frac{6}{5}$	Ⓖ	Ⓗ
$\frac{1}{2} + \frac{1}{4} + \frac{2}{5} = \frac{4}{11}$	Ⓘ	Ⓙ

 ©Curriculum Associates, LLC Copying is not permitted

5 Write the decimal below in standard form.

$$2 \times 10 + 6 \times 1 + 5 \times \frac{1}{10} + 7 \times \frac{1}{100} + 4 \times \frac{1}{1,000}$$

···

6 It snowed $5\frac{1}{2}$ inches in January and $4\frac{7}{8}$ inches in February. How many more inches did it snow in January than in February?

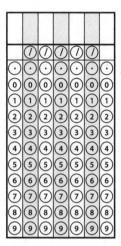

7 Write $>$, $<$, $=$ to compare the decimals.

a. 6.104 ◯ 6.106

b. 6.079 ◯ 5.793

c. 5.785 ◯ 5.793

d. 6.106 ◯ 6.079

8 Ben is learning about place value in his math class. He writes these two numbers.

74,443   3.557

Choose the correct word to fill in each blank below.

The value of the 4 in the hundreds place is 10 times the value of the 4 in the _____ place.

Ⓐ ones

Ⓑ tens

Ⓒ thousands

The value of the 5 in the _____ place is $\frac{1}{10}$ the value of the 5 in the tenths place.

Ⓐ ones

Ⓑ hundredths

Ⓒ thousandth

Performance Task

Answer the questions and show all your work on separate paper.

You have a movie theater gift card worth $40, so you invite a friend to go to the movies with you. Your friend challenges you to spend the exact value of the gift card. Find at least one way to do so by choosing from the items listed below.

Item	Price
2D Movie Ticket	$7.25
3D Movie Ticket	$8.50
Small Popcorn	$3.25
Medium Popcorn	$5.50
Large Popcorn	$7.75
Bottle of Water	$2.50
1 Ounce of Snack Mix	$0.50

Checklist

Did you . . .

☐ organize your choices?

☐ check your calculations?

☐ use words and numbers to complete the task?

REFLECT

Use Mathematical Practices After you complete the task, choose one of the following questions to answer.

• **Persevere** What strategies did you use? If a strategy did not work, what did you do?

• **Model** How did you use equations to solve this problem?

©Curriculum Associates, LLC   Copying is not permitted

Draw or write to show examples for each term. Then draw or write to show other math words in the unit.

base (of a power) in a power, the number that is used as a repeated factor.

My Example

base ten a ten-digit number system in which the value of a digit depends on its place. The value of each place is 10 times the value of the place to the right and $\frac{1}{10}$ of the value of the place to the left.

My Example

common denominator a number that is a common multiple of the denominators of two or more fractions.

My Example

decimal a number containing a decimal point that separates a whole from fractional place values (tenths, hundredths, thousandths, and so on).

My Example

expanded form a way to write a number to show the place value of each digit.
For example, $34.56 = 3 \times 10 + 4 \times 1 + 5 \times \frac{1}{10} + 6 \times \frac{1}{100}$.

My Example

exponent the number in a power that tells how many times to use the base as a factor in repeated multiplication.

My Example

inequality a mathematical statement that uses an inequality symbol ($<$ or $>$) to show the relationship between expressions with different values.

My Example

power of 10 a number that can be written as a product of tens. For example, 100 and 1,000 are powers of 10 because $100 = 10 \times 10$ and $1,000 = 10 \times 10 \times 10$.

My Example

thousandths the parts formed when a whole is divided into 1,000 equal parts.

My Example

My Word: _____

_____

_____

My Example

My Word: _____

_____

_____

My Example

My Word: _____

_____

_____

My Example

  ©Curriculum Associates, LLC   Copying is not permitted.

English	Español	Example/Ejemplo
Aa		

acute angle an angle that measures more than 0° but less than 90°.

ángulo agudo ángulo que mide más de 0° pero menos de 90°.

---

acute triangle a triangle that has three acute angles.

triángulo acutángulo triángulo que tiene tres ángulos agudos.

---

addend a number being added.

sumando número que se suma.

$$24 + 35 = 59$$
addends

---

algorithm a set of routine steps used to solve problems.

algoritmo conjunto de pasos que se siguen rutinariamente para resolver problemas.

$$
\begin{array}{r}
17 \text{ R } 19 \\
31\overline{)546} \\
31 \downarrow \\
\overline{236} \\
217 \\
\overline{19}
\end{array}
$$

AM the time from midnight until before noon.

a. m. el tiempo que transcurre desde la medianoche hasta el mediodía.

AM 7:20

---

angle a geometric shape formed by two rays, lines, or line segments that meet at a common point.

ángulo figura geométrica formada por dos semirrectas, rectas o segmentos de recta que se encuentran en un punto.

C
A   B

English	Español	Example/Ejemplo
area the amount of space inside a closed two-dimensional figure. Area is measured in square units such as square centimeters.	**área** cantidad de espacio dentro de una figura bidimensional cerrada. El área se mide en unidades cuadradas, como los centímetros cuadrados.	Area = 4 square units
array a set of objects arranged in equal rows and equal columns.	**matriz** conjunto de objetos agrupados en filas y columnas iguales.	
associative property of addition when the grouping of three or more addends is changed, the total does not change.	**propiedad asociativa de la suma** cambiar la agrupación de tres o más sumandos no cambia el total.	$(2 + 3) + 4 = 2 + (3 + 4)$
associative property of multiplication changing the grouping of three or more factors does not change the product.	**propiedad asociativa de la multiplicación** cambiar la agrupación de tres o más factores no cambia el producto.	$(2 \times 4) \times 3 = 2 \times (4 \times 3)$
attribute any characteristic of an object or shape, such as number of sides or angles, lengths of sides, or angle measures.	**atributo** característica de un objeto o una figura, como el número de lados o ángulos, la longitud de los lados o la medida de los ángulos.	attributes of a square: • 4 square corners • 4 sides of equal length
axis a horizontal or vertical number line that determines a coordinate plane. The plural form is *axes*.	**eje** recta numérica horizontal o vertical que determina un plano de coordenadas.	*y*-axis, *x*-axis

Bb

base (of a power) in a power, the number that is used as a repeated factor.	**base (de una potencia)** en una potencia, el número que se usa como factor repetido.	8^2

©Curriculum Associates, LLC   Copying is not permitted

English	Español	Example/Ejemplo
base (of a prism) one side of a prism, usually considered to be the side shown as the bottom of the prism. In the volume formula $V = B \times h$, B represents the area of the base of the prism.	**base (de un prisma)** lado de un prisma (por lo general, el lado inferior). En la fórmula de volumen $V = B \times a$, B representa el área de la base del prisma.	base
base ten a ten-digit number system in which the value of a digit depends on its place. The value of each place is 10 times the value of the place to the right and $\frac{1}{10}$ of the value of the place to the left.	**base diez** sistema numérico en el que el valor de un dígito depende de su valor posicional. El valor de cada posición es 10 veces el valor de la posición que está a la derecha y $\frac{1}{10}$ del valor de la posición que está a la izquierda.	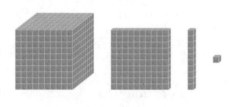
benchmark fraction a common fraction that you might compare other fractions to.	**fracción de referencia** fracción común que se puede comparar con otras fracciones.	$\frac{1}{4}, \frac{1}{2}, \frac{2}{3},$ and $\frac{3}{4}$ are often used as benchmark fractions.

Cc

English	Español	Example/Ejemplo
capacity the amount a container can hold. Capacity can be measured in the same units as liquid volume.	**capacidad** cantidad que cabe en un recipiente. La capacidad se mide en las mismas unidades que el volumen líquido.	 capacity of 2 liters
category a collection of objects grouped together based on attributes they have in common.	**categoría** grupo de objetos clasificados según atributos que tienen en común.	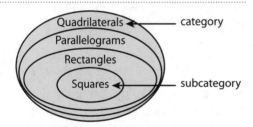
centimeter (cm) a unit of length. There are 100 centimeters in 1 meter.	**centímetro (cm)** unidad de longitud. 100 centímetros equivalen a 1 metro.	Your little finger is about 1 **centimeter** (cm) across. 

©Curriculum Associates, LLC   Copying is not permitted

English	Español	Example/Ejemplo
closed figure a two-dimensional figure that begins and ends at the same point.	**figura cerrada** figura bidimensional que comienza y termina en el mismo punto. amounts, or	Closed figure Open figure
column a vertical line of objects or numbers, such as in an array or table.	**columna** línea vertical de objetos, como las de una matriz o una tabla.	
common denominator a number that is a common multiple of the denominators of two or more fractions.	**denominadores communes** número que es común múltiplo de los denominadores de dos o más fracciones.	$2 \times 3 = 6$, so 6 is a common denominator for $3\frac{1}{2}$ and $1\frac{1}{3}$.
commutative property of addition changing the order of addends does not change the total.	**propiedad conmutativa de la suma** cambiar el orden de los sumandos no cambia el total.	$3 + 4$ $=$ $4 + 3$
commutative property of multiplication changing the order of the factors does not change the product.	**propiedad conmutativa de la multiplicación** cambiar el orden de los factores no cambia el producto.	3×2 $=$ 2×3
compare to decide if numbers, amounts, or sizes are *greater than*, *less than*, or *equal to* each other.	**comparar** determinar si un número, una cantidad o un tamaño es *mayor que, menor que* o *igual a* otro número, otra cantidad u otro tamaño.	$3.37 > 3.096$
compose to make by combining parts. You can put together numbers to make a greater number or shapes to make a new shape.	**componer** combinar partes para formar algo. Se pueden combinar números para formar un número mayor o figuras para formar otra figura.	50° 50° 50° The three 50° angles compose the larger angle.
composite number a number that has more than one pair of factors.	**número compuesto** número que tiene más de un par de factores.	16 is a composite number.

©Curriculum Associates, LLC   Copying is not permitted

English	Español	Example/Ejemplo
convert to write an equivalent measurement using a different unit.	**convertir** expresar una medida equivalente en una unidad diferente.	5 feet = 60 inches
coordinate plane a two-dimensional space formed by two perpendicular number lines called *axes*.	**plano de coordenadas** espacio bidimensional formado por dos rectas numéricas perpendiculares llamadas *ejes*.	**Coordinate Plane**
corresponding terms terms that have the same position in two related patterns. For example, the second term in one pattern and the second term in a related pattern are corresponding terms.	**términos correspondientes** términos que tienen la misma posición en dos patrones relacionados. Por ejemplo, el segundo término de un patrón y el segundo término de un patrón relacionado son términos correspondientes.	Pattern A: 6, **9**, 12, 15, 18 Pattern B: 12, **18**, 24, 30, 36
cubic unit the volume of a unit cube.	**unidad cúbica** el volumen de un cubo con aristas de 1 unidad de longitud.	 1 unit 1 unit ← 1 unit →
cup (c) a unit of liquid volume in the customary system. 4 cups is equal to 1 quart.	**taza (tz)** unidad de volumen líquido del sistema usual. 4 tazas equivalen a 1 cuarto.	 cup

English	Español	Example/Ejemplo

customary system the measurement system commonly used in the United States that measures length in inches, feet, yards, and miles; liquid volume in cups, pints, quarts, and gallons; and weight in ounces and pounds.

sistema usual sistema de medición comúnmente usado en Estados Unidos. La longitud se mide en pulgadas, pies, yardas, y millas; el volumen líquido, en tazas, pintas, cuartos, y galones; y el peso, en onzas y libras.

Length
1 foot = 12 inches
1 yard = 3 feet
1 mile = 5,280 feet
Weight
1 pound = 16 ounces
Liquid Volume
1 quart = 2 pints
1 quart = 4 cups
1 gallon = 4 quarts

Dd

data a set of collected information. Often numerical information such as a list of measurements.

datos conjunto de información reunida. A menudo es información numérica, tal como una lista de mediciones.

earthworm lengths (in inches):
$4\frac{1}{2}, 5, 5, 5, 5\frac{1}{4}, 5\frac{1}{4}, 5\frac{1}{4}, 6, 6\frac{1}{4}$

decimal a number containing a decimal point that separates a whole from fractional place values (tenths, hundredths, thousandths, and so on).

número decimal número que contiene un punto decimal que separa la posición de las unidades de las posiciones fraccionarias (décimas, centésimas, milésimas, etc.).

1.293

decimal point the dot used in a decimal that separates the ones place from the tenths place.

punto decimal punto que se usa en un número decimal para separar la posición de las unidades de la posición de las décimas.

1.65
↑
decimal point

decompose to break into parts. You can break apart numbers and shapes.

descomponer separar en partes. Se pueden separar en partes números y figuras.

$\frac{3}{8} = \frac{1}{8} + \frac{1}{8} + \frac{1}{8}$

degree (°) a unit used to measure angles. There are 360° in a circle.

grado (°) unidad que se usa para medir ángulos. Un círculo mide 360°.

There are 360° in a circle.

©Curriculum Associates, LLC Copying is not permitted

English	Español	Example/Ejemplo
denominator the number below the line in a fraction that tells the number of equal parts in the whole.	**denominador** número que está debajo de la línea de una fracción. Dice cuántas partes iguales hay en el entero.	$\frac{2}{3}$
difference the result of subtraction.	**diferencia** el resultado de la resta.	$\begin{array}{r} 16.75 \\ -\ 15.70 \\ \hline \textbf{1.05} \end{array}$
digit a symbol used to write numbers.	**dígito** símbolo que se usa para escribir números.	The digits are 0, 1, 2, 3, 4, 5, 6, 7, 8, and 9.
dimension length in one direction. A figure may have one, two, or three dimensions.	**dimension** longitud en una dirección. Una figura puede tener una, dos o tres dimensiones.	5 in. 2 in. 3 in.
distribution how spread out or how clustered pieces of data are.	**distribución** qué tan esparcidos o agrupados están los datos.	Most of the data are clustered between $\frac{1}{8}$ and $\frac{1}{2}$. Tomato Weight (pounds)
distributive property when one of the factors of a product is written as a sum, multiplying each addend by the other factor before adding does not change the product.	**propiedad distributiva** cuando uno de los factores de un producto se escribe como suma, multiplicar cada sumando por el otro factor antes de sumar no cambia el producto.	$2 \times (3 + 6) = (2 \times 3) + (2 \times 6)$
divide to separate into equal groups and find the number in each group or the number of groups.	**divisor** separar en grupos iguales y hallar cuántos hay en cada grupo o el número de grupos.	$2{,}850 \div 38 = 75$
dividend the number that is divided by another number.	**dividendo** el número que se divide por otro número.	$15 \div 3 = 5$

©Curriculum Associates, LLC   Copying is not permitted

English	Español	Example/Ejemplo
division an operation used to separate a number of items into equal-sized groups.	**división** operación que se usa para separar una cantidad de objetos en grupos iguales.	**Division** $12 \div 3 = 4$ total, number of groups, number in each group
divisor the number by which another number is divided.	**divisor** el número por el que se divide otro número.	$15 \div 3 = 5$

Ee

English	Español	Example/Ejemplo
edge a line segment where two faces meet in a three-dimensional shape.	**arista** segmento de recta donde se encuentran dos caras de una figura tridimensional.	edge
elapsed time the amount of time that has passed between a start time and an end time.	**tiempo transcurrido** tiempo que ha pasado entre el momento de inicio y el fin.	The elapsed time from 2:00 PM to 3:00 PM is 1 hour.
equal having the same value, same size, or same amount.	**igual** que tiene el mismo valor, el mismo tamaño o la misma cantidad.	$25 + 15 = 40$ $25 + 15$ **is equal to** 40.
equal sign (=) a symbol that means *is the same value as.*	**signo de igual (=)** símbolo que significa *tiene el mismo valor que.*	$12 + 4 = 16$
equation a mathematical statement that uses an equal sign (=) to show that two expressions have the same value.	**ecuación** enunciado matemático que tiene un signo de igual (=) para mostrar que dos expresiones tienen el mismo valor.	$25 - 15 = 10$
equilateral triangle a triangle that has all three sides the same length.	**triángulo equilátero** triángulo que tiene los tres lados de igual longitud.	8 in. 8 in. 8 in.

 ©Curriculum Associates, LLC Copying is not permitted

English	Español	Example/Ejemplo
equivalent fractions two or more different fractions that name the same part of a whole or the same point on a number line.	**fracciones equivalentes** dos o más fracciones diferentes que nombran la misma parte de un entero y el mismo punto en una recta numérica.	$\dfrac{2}{4} = \dfrac{1}{2}$ $\dfrac{5}{10} = \dfrac{1}{2}$
estimate (noun) a close guess made using mathematical thinking.	**estimación** suposición aproximada que se hace usando el razonamiento matemático.	$28 + 21 = ?$ $30 + 20 = 50$ 50 is an estimate of the sum.
estimate (verb) to make a close guess based on mathematical thinking.	**estimar / hacer una estimación** hacer una suposición aproximada usando el razonamiento matemático.	$415 \div 20$ is about 21.
evaluate to find the value of an expression.	**evaluar** hallar el valor de una expresión.	The expression $48 \div (6 + 10)$ has a value of 3.
even number a whole number that always has 0, 2, 4, 6, or 8 in the ones place. An even number of objects can be put into pairs or into two equal groups without any leftovers.	**número par** número entero que siempre tiene 0, 2, 4, 6, o 8 en la posición de las unidades. Un número par de objetos puede agruparse en pares o en dos grupos iguales sin que queden sobrantes.	20, 22, 24, 26, and 28 are even numbers.
expanded form a way to write a number to show the place value of each digit.	**forma desarrollada** manera de escribir un número para mostrar el valor posicional de cada dígito.	$34.56 = 3 \times 10 + 4 \times 1 + 5 + \dfrac{1}{10} + 6 \times \dfrac{1}{100}$
exponent the number in a power that tells how many times to use the base as a factor in repeated multiplication.	**exponente** el número de una potencia que dice cuántas veces debe multiplicarse la base.	8^2

English	Español	Example/Ejemplo
expression one or more numbers, unknown numbers, and/or operation symbols that represents a quantity.	**expresión** uno o más números, números desconocidos, o símbolos de operaciones que representan una cantidad.	3×4 or $5 + b$

Ff

English	Español	Example/Ejemplo
face a flat surface of a solid shape.	**cara** superficie plana de una figura sólida.	face
fact family a group of related equations that use the same numbers, but in a different order, and two different operation symbols. A fact family can show the relationship between addition and subtraction or between multiplication and division.	**familia de datos** grupo de ecuaciones relacionadas que tienen los mismos números, ordenados de distinta manera, y dos símbolos de operaciones diferentes. Una familia de datos puede mostrar la relación que existe entre la multiplicación y la división.	$5 \times 4 = 20$ $4 \times 5 = 20$ $20 \div 4 = 5$ $20 \div 5 = 4$
factor a number that is multiplied.	**factor** número que se multiplica.	$4 \times 5 = 20$ factors
factor pair two numbers that are multiplied together to give a product.	**pares de factores** dos números que se multiplican para obtener un producto.	$4 \times 5 = 20$ factor pair
factors of a number whole numbers that multiply together to get the given number.	**factores de un número** números enteros que se multiplican para obtener el número dado.	$4 \times 5 = 20$ 4 and 5 are factors of 20.
flow chart a diagram that uses arrows to show how sets of numbers or objects are related.	**diagrama de árbol** un diagrama que contiene líneas que se conectan para mostrar relaciones entre números u objetos.	**Triangles** Scalene Isosceles Equilateral
foot (ft) a unit of length in the customary system. There are 12 inches in 1 foot.	**pie (ft)** unidad de longitud del sistema usual. Un pie equivale a 12 pulgadas.	12 inches = 1 foot

©Curriculum Associates, LLC   Copying is not permitted

English	Español	Example/Ejemplo
formula a mathematical relationship that is expressed in the form of an equation.	**formula** relación matemática que se expresa en forma de ecuación.	$A = \ell \times w$

Gg

English	Español	Example/Ejemplo
gallon (gal) a unit of liquid volume in the customary system. There are 4 quarts in 1 gallon.	**galón (gal)** unidad de volumen líquido del sistema usual. 1 galón es igual a 4 cuartos.	4 quarts = 1 gallon
gram (g) a unit of mass in the metric system. A paper clip has a mass of about 1 gram. There are 1,000 grams in 1 kilogram.	**gramo (g)** unidad de masa del sistema métrico. Un clip tiene una masa de aproximadamente 1 gramo. 1,000 gramos equivalen a 1 kilogramo.	1,000 grams = 1 kilogram
greater than symbol (>) a symbol used to compare two numbers when the first is greater than the second.	**símbolo de mayor que (>)** símbolo que se usa para comparar dos números cuando el primero es mayor que el segundo.	$3.37 > 3.096$
grouping symbols a symbol, such as braces { }, brackets [ ], or parentheses ( ), used to group parts of an expression that should be evaluated before others.	**símbolos de agrupación** símbolos, tales como las llaves { }, los corchetes [ ], o los paréntesis ( ), que se usan para agrupar partes de una expresión que deben evaluarse antes que otras.	$3 + (5 \times 3) = 3 + 15$ $3 + \{5 \times 3\} = 3 + 15$ $3 + [5 \times 3] = 3 + 15$

Hh

English	Español	Example/Ejemplo
hexagon a polygon with exactly 6 sides and 6 angles.	**hexágono** polígono que tiene exactamente 6 lados y 6 ángulos.	
hierarchy a ranking of categories based on attributes.	**jerarquía** clasificación por categorías basada en atributos.	Quadrilaterals / Parallelograms / Rectangles / Squares
hour (h) a unit of time. There are 60 minutes in 1 hour.	**hora (h)** unidad de tiempo. 1 hora equivale a 60 minutos.	60 minutes = 1 hour

©Curriculum Associates, LLC   Copying is not permitted

English	Español	Example/Ejemplo
hundredths the parts formed when a whole is divided into 100 equal parts.	**centésimos (fracciones)/ centésimas (decimales)** partes que se forman cuando un entero se divide en 100 partes iguales.	

Ii

English	Español	Example/Ejemplo
inch (in.) a unit of length in the customary system. There are 12 inches in 1 foot.	**pulgada (pulg.)** unidad de longitud del sistema usual. 12 pulgadas equivalen a 1 pie.	The length of a quarter is about 1 **inch** (in.).
inequality a mathematical statement that uses an inequality symbol (< or >) to show the relationship between expressions with different values.	**desigualdad** enunciado matemático en el que se usa un signo de desigualdad (< o >) para mostrar que dos expresiones tienen valores diferentes.	$3.275 > 3.240$ $3.240 < 3.275$
inverse operations operations that undo each other. For example, addition and subtraction are inverse operations, and multiplication and division are inverse operations.	**operación inversa** operaciones que se anulan unas a otras. Por ejemplo, la suma y la resta son operaciones inversas, y la multiplicación y la división son operaciones inversas.	$3{,}000 \div 10 = 300$ $300 \times 10 = 3{,}000$
isosceles triangle a triangle that has at least two sides the same length.	**triángulo isósceles** triángulo que tiene al menos dos lados de igual longitud.	8 in. 8 in. 6 in.

Kk

English	Español	Example/Ejemplo
kilogram (kg) a unit of mass in the metric system. There are 1,000 grams in 1 kilogram.	**kilogramo (kg)** unidad de masa del sistema métrico. 1 kilogramo equivale a 1,000 gramos.	1,000 grams = 1 kilogram

©Curriculum Associates, LLC Copying is not permitted

English	Español	Example/Ejemplo
kilometer (km) a unit of length in the metric system. There are 1,000 meters in 1 kilometer.	**kilómetro (km)** unidad de longitud del sistema métrico. 1 kilómetro equivale a 1,000 metros.	1 kilometer = 1,000 meters

Ll

English	Español	Example/Ejemplo
length measurement that tells the distance from one point to another, or how long something is.	**longitud** medida que indica la distancia de un punto a otro, o cuán largo es un objeto.	length
less than symbol (<) a symbol used to compare two numbers when the first is less than the second.	**símbolo de menor que (<)** símbolo que se usa para comparar dos números cuando el primero es menor que el segundo.	$3.096 < 3.37$
line a straight row of points that goes on forever in both directions.	**recta** fila recta de puntos que continúa infinitamente en ambas direcciones.	
line of symmetry a line that divides a shape into two mirror images.	**eje de simetría** recta que divide una figura en dos imágenes reflejadas.	
line plot a data display that shows data as marks above a number line.	**diagrama de puntos** representación de datos en la cual se muestran los datos como marcas sobre una recta numérica.	**Sea Lion Lengths** 48 49 50 51 52 **Inches**
line segment a straight row of points that starts at one point and ends at another point.	**segmento de recta** fila recta de puntos que comienza en un punto y termina en otro punto.	A B
liquid volume the amount of space a liquid takes up.	**volumen líquido** cantidad de espacio que ocupa un líquido.	When you measure how much water is in a bucket, you measure liquid volume.
liter (L) a unit of liquid volume in the metric system. There are 1,000 milliliters in 1 liter.	**litro (l)** unidad de volumen líquido del sistema métrico. 1 litro equivale a 1,000 mililitros.	1,000 milliliters = 1 liter

English	Español	Example/Ejemplo

Mm

English	Español	Example/Ejemplo
mass the amount of matter in an object. Measuring the mass of an object is one way to measure how heavy it is. Units of mass include the gram and kilogram.	**masa** cantidad de materia que hay en un objeto. Medir la masa de un objeto es una manera de medir qué tan pesado es. El gramo y el kilogramo son unidades de masa.	The mass of a paper clip is about 1 gram.
meter (m) a unit of length in the metric system. There are 100 centimeters in 1 meter.	**metro (m)** unidad de longitud del sistema métrico. 1 metro es igual a 100 centímetros.	100 centimeters = 1 meter
metric system the measurement system that measures length based on meters, liquid volume based on liters, and mass based on grams.	**sistema métrico** sistema de medición. La longitud se mide en metros; el volumen líquido, en litros; y la masa, en gramos.	

Length
1 kilometer = 1,000 meters
1 meter = 100 centimeters
1 meter = 1,000 millimeters

Mass
1 kilogram = 1,000 grams

Volume
1 liter = 1,000 milliliters

English	Español	Example/Ejemplo
mile (mi) a unit of length in the customary system. There are 5,280 feet in 1 mile.	**milla** unidad de longitud del sistema usual. 1 milla equivale a 5,280 pies.	5,280 feet = 1 mile
milliliter (ml) a unit of liquid volume in the metric system. There are 1,000 milliliters in 1 liter.	**mililitro (ml)** unidad de volumen líquido del sistema métrico. 1,000 mililitros equivalen a 1 litro.	1,000 milliliters = 1 liter
millimeter (mm) a unit of length in the metric system. There 1,000 millimeters in 1 meter.	**milímetro (mm)** unidad de longitud del sistema métrico. 1,000 milímetros equivalen a 1 metro.	1,000 millimeters = 1 meter

©Curriculum Associates, LLC   Copying is not permitted

English	Español	Example/Ejemplo
minute (min) a unit of time. There are 60 minutes in 1 hour.	**minuto (min)** unidad de tiempo. 60 minutos equivalen a 1 hora.	60 minutes = 1 hour
mixed number a number with a whole number part and a fractional part.	**número mixto** número con una parte entera y una parte fraccionaria.	$2\frac{3}{8}$
multiple the product of a given number and any other whole number.	**múltiplo** producto de un número y cualquier otro número entero.	4, 8, 12, 16, and so on, are multiples of 4.
multiplication an operation used to find the total number of items in a given number of equal-sized groups. See also *multiplicative comparison*.	**multiplicación** operación que se usa para hallar el número total de objetos en un número dado de grupos de igual tamaño. Ver también la *comparación multiplicativa*.	**Multiplication** $3 \times 4 = 12$ number of groups · · · number in each group · · · total
multiplicative comparison a comparison that tells how many times as many.	**comparación multiplicative** comparación que dice cuántas veces una cantidad es otra cantidad.	$\frac{1}{2} \times 6 = 3$ tells that 3 is $\frac{1}{2}$ as many as 6, and that 3 is 6 times as many as $\frac{1}{2}$.
multiply to repeatedly add the same number a certain number of times. Used to find the total number of items in equal-sized groups.	**multiplicar** sumar el mismo número una y otra vez una cierta cantidad de veces. Se multiplica para hallar el número total de objetos que hay en grupos de igual tamaño.	42 36 30 24 18 12 6 $6 \times 7 = 42$

Nn

English	Español	Example/Ejemplo
numerator the number above the line in a fraction that tells the number of equal parts that are being described.	**numerador** número que está encima de la línea de una fracción. Dice cuántas partes iguales se describen.	$\frac{2}{3}$

©Curriculum Associates, LLC   Copying is not permitted

English	Español	Example/Ejemplo

Oo

obtuse angle an angle that measures more than 90° but less than 180°.	**ángulo obtuso** ángulo que mide más de 90° pero menos de 180°.	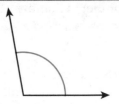
obtuse triangle a triangle that has one obtuse angle.	**triángulo obtusángulo** triángulo que tiene un ángulo obtuso.	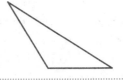
odd number a whole number that always has 1, 3, 5, 7, or 9 in the ones place. An odd number of objects cannot be put into pairs or into two equal groups without a leftover.	**número impar** número entero que siempre tiene el dígito 1, 3, 5, 7, o 9 en el lugar de las unidades. Los números impares no pueden ordenarse en pares o en dos grupos iguales sin sobrantes.	21, 23, 25, 27, and 29 are odd numbers.
operation a mathematical action such as addition, subtraction, multiplication, or division.	**operación** acción matemática como la suma, la resta, la multiplicación y la división.	$15 + 5 = 20$ $20 - 5 = 15$ $4 \times 6 = 24$ $24 \div 6 = 4$
ordered pair a pair of numbers, (x, y), that describes the location of a point in the coordinate plane, where the x-coordinate gives the point's horizontal distance from the origin, and the y-coordinate gives the point's vertical distance from the origin.	**par ordenado** par de números, (x, y), que describen la ubicación de un punto en el plano de coordenadas. La coordenada x indica la distancia horizontal del punto al origen, y la coordenada y indica la distancia vertical del punto al origen.	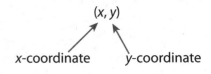
origin the point (0, 0) in the coordinate plane where the x-axis and y-axis intersect.	**origen** el punto (0, 0) en el plano de coordenadas, donde se intersecan el eje x y el eje y.	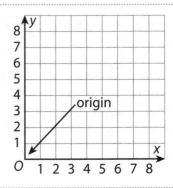

©Curriculum Associates, LLC   Copying is not permitted

English	Español	Example/Ejemplo
ounce (oz) a unit of weight in the customary system. A slice of bread weighs about 1 ounce. There are 16 ounces in 1 pound.	**onza (oz)** unidad de peso del sistema usual. Una rebanada de pan pesa aproximadamente 1 onza. 16 onzas equivalen a 1 libra.	16 ounces = 1 pound

Pp

English	Español	Example/Ejemplo
parallel lines lines that are always the same distance apart and never cross.	**rectas paralelas** rectas que siempre están a la misma distancia y nunca se cruzan.	
parallelogram a quadrilateral with opposite sides parallel and equal in length.	**paralelogramo** cuadrilátero que tiene lados opuestos paralelos e iguales en longitud.	
partial products the products you get in each step of the partial-products strategy. You use place value to find partial products.	**productos parciales** los productos que se obtienen en cada paso de la estrategia de productos parciales. Se usa el valor posicional para hallar productos parciales.	The partial products for 124×3 are 3×100 or 300, 3×20 or 60, and 3×4 or 12.
partial quotients The quotients you get in each step of the partial-quotients strategy. You use place value to find partial quotients.	**cocientes parciales** los cocientes que se obtienen en cada paso de la estrategia de cocientes parciales. Se usa el valor posicional para hallar cocientes parciales.	The partial quotients for $2{,}124 \div 4$ are $2{,}000 \div 4$ or 500, $100 \div 4$ or 25, and $24 \div 4$ or 6.
partial sums the sums you get in each step of the partial-sums strategy. You use place value to find partial sums.	**sumas parciales** las sumas que se obtienen en cada paso de la estrategia de sumas parciales. Se usa el valor posicional para hallar sumas parciales.	The partial sums for $124 + 234$ are $100 + 200$ or 300, $20 + 30$ or 50, and $4 + 4$ or 8.
partial-products strategy a strategy used to multiply multi-digit numbers.	**estrategia de productos parciales** estrategia que se usa para multiplicar números de varios dígitos.	$$\begin{array}{r} 218 \\ \times\ 6 \\ \hline 48 \ \ (6 \times 8 \text{ ones}) \\ 60 \ \ (6 \times 1 \text{ ten}) \\ 1200 \ \ (6 \times 2 \text{ hundreds}) \\ \hline 1308 \end{array}$$

©Curriculum Associates, LLC   Copying is not permitted

English	Español	Example/Ejemplo
partial-quotients strategy a strategy used to divide multi-digit numbers.	**estrategia de cocientes parciales** estrategia que se usa para dividir números de varios dígitos.	6 25 500 4)2,125 − 2,000 125 − 100 25 − 24 1 The partial quotients are 500, 25, and 6. The quotient, 531, is the sum of the partial quotients. The remainder is 1.
partial-sums strategy a strategy used to add multi-digit numbers.	**estrategia de sumas parciales** estrategia que se usa para sumar números de varios dígitos.	312 +235 **Add the hundreds.** 500 **Add the tens.** 40 **Add the ones.** 7 547
pattern a series of numbers or shapes that follow a rule to repeat or change. See also *terms of a pattern*.	**patrón** serie de números o figuras que siguen una regla para repetirse o cambiar. Ver también *términos de un patrón*.	
pentagon a polygon with exactly 5 sides and 5 angles.	**pentágono** polígono con que tiene exactamente 5 lados y 5 ángulos.	
perimeter the distance around a two-dimensional shape. The perimeter is equal to the sum of the lengths of the sides.	**perímetro** longitud del contorno de una figura bidimensional. El perímetro es igual al total de las longitudes de los lados.	60 yards 40 yards / 40 yards 60 yards The perimeter of the soccer field is 200 yards. (60 yd + 40 yd + 60 yd + 40 yd)

©Curriculum Associates, LLC   Copying is not permitted

English	Español	Example/Ejemplo
period a group of three places in a number, usually separated by commas. The first three periods are the ones period, the thousands period, and the millions period.	**período** grupo de tres valores posicionales de un número, generalmente separados por comas. Los primeros tres períodos son el período de las unidades, el período de los millares y el período de los millones.	321,987 987 is the first period.
perpendicular lines two lines that meet to form a right angle, or a 90° angle.	**rectas perpendiculars** dos rectas que se unen para formar un ángulo recto, o un ángulo de 90°	
pint (pt) a unit of liquid volume in the customary system. There are 2 cups in 1 pint.	**pinta (pt)** unidad de volumen líquido del sistema usual. 1 pinta equivale a 2 tazas.	2 cups = 1 pint
place value the value of a digit based on its position in a number.	**valor posicional** valor de un dígito según su posición en un número.	The **2** in 3.52 is in the **hundredths** place and has a value of **2 hundredths** or 0.02.
plane figure a two-dimensional figure, such as a circle, triangle, or rectangle.	**figura plana** figura bidimensional, como un círculo, triángulo o rectángulo.	
PM the time from noon until before midnight.	**p. m.** tiempo que transcurre desde el mediodía hasta la medianoche.	PM 5:10
point a single location in space.	**punto** ubicación única en el espacio.	*A* ●
polygon a two-dimensional closed figure made with three or more straight line segments that do not cross over each other.	**polígono** figura bidimensional cerrada formada que tiene tres o más segmentos de recta que no se cruzan.	Polygons / Not Polygons
pound (lb) a unit of weight in the customary system. There are 16 ounces in 1 pound.	**libra (lb)** unidad de peso del sistema usual. 1 libra equivale a 16 onzas.	16 ounces = 1 pound

©Curriculum Associates, LLC   Copying is not permitted

English	Español	Example/Ejemplo
power of 10 a number that can be written as a product of tens.	**potencia de 10** número que puede escribirse como producto de decenas.	100 and 1,000 are powers of 10 because $100 = 10 \times 10$ and $1,000 = 10 \times 10 \times 10$.
prime number a whole number greater than 1 whose only factors are 1 and itself.	**número primo** número entero mayor que 1 cuyos únicos factores son 1 y él mismo.	2, 3, 5, 7, 11, 13, 17, 19 are prime numbers.
product the result of multiplication.	**producto** el resultado de la multiplicación.	$5 \times 3 = 15$
protractor a tool used to measure angles.	**transportador** herramienta que se usa para medir ángulos.	

Qq

quadrilateral a polygon with exactly 4 sides and 4 angles.	**cuadrilátero** polígono que tiene exactamente 4 lados y 4 ángulos.	
quart (qt) a unit of liquid volume in the customary system. There are 4 cups in 1 quart.	**cuarto (ct)** unidad de volumen líquido del sistema usual. 1 cuarto equivale a 4 tazas.	4 cups = 1 quart
quotient the result of division.	**cociente** el resultado de la división.	$15 \div 3 = 5$

Rr

ray a straight row of points that starts at one point and goes on forever in one direction.	**semirrecta** fila recta de puntos que comienza en un punto y continúa infinitamente en una dirección.	$A \quad\quad B$
rectangular prism a solid figure with 6 rectangular faces.	**prisma rectangular** figura sólida con seis caras rectangulares.	

©Curriculum Associates, LLC   Copying is not permitted

English	Español	Example/Ejemplo
regroup to compose or decompose tens, hundreds, thousands, and so forth.	**reagrupar** componer o descomponer decenas, centenas, millares, etc.	10 tenths can be regrouped as 1 whole, or 1 tenth can be regrouped as 10 hundredths.
remainder the amount left over when one number does not divide another number a whole number of times.	**residuo** en la división, la cantidad que queda después de haber formado grupos iguales.	Remainder $17 \div 5 = 3 \text{ R } 2$
rhombus a quadrilateral with all sides the same length.	**rombo** cuadrilátero con todos los lados de la misma longitud.	
right angle an angle that looks like a square corner and measures 90°.	**ángulo recto** ángulo que parece la esquina de un cuadrado y mide 90°.	90°
right triangle a triangle that has one right angle.	**triángulo rectángulo** triángulo con un ángulo recto.	90°
round to find a number that is close in value to a given number by finding the nearest ten, hundred, or other place value.	**redondear** hallar un número que es cercano en valor al número dado hallando la decena, la centena o otro valor posicional más cercano.	48 rounded to the nearest ten is 50.
row a horizontal line of objects or number, such as in an array or table.	**fila** línea horizontal de objetos o números, tal como las que aparecen en una matriz o una tabla.	★ ★ ★ ★ ★ ★ ★ ★ ★ ★ ★ ★ ★ ★ ★
rule a procedure that is followed to go from one number or shape to the next in a pattern.	**regla** procedimiento que se sigue para ir de un número o una figura al número o la figura siguiente de un patrón.	17, 22, 27, 32, 37, 42 rule: add 5

©Curriculum Associates, LLC   Copying is not permitted

English	Español	Example/Ejemplo

Ss

scale (on a graph) the value represented by the distance between one tick mark and the next on a number line.

escala (en una gráfica) el valor que representa la distancia entre una marca y la marca siguiente de una recta numérica.

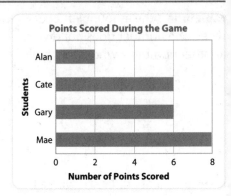

scalene triangle a triangle that has no sides the same length.

triángulo escaleno triángulo que no tiene lados de igual longitud.

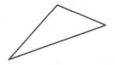

scaling resizing a quantity by multiplying by a factor.

poner a escala cambiar de tamaño una cantidad multiplicándola por un factor.

	Words	Symbols
stretching	6 doubled is 12.	$2 \times 6 = 12$
shrinking	Half of 6 is 3.	$\frac{1}{2} \times 6 = 3$

second (s) a unit of time. There are 60 seconds in 1 minute.

segundo (s) unidad de tiempo. Sesenta segundos equivalen a 1 minuto.

60 seconds = 1 minute

side a line segment that forms part of a two-dimensional shape.

lado segmento de recta que forma parte de una figura bidimensional.

side

solid figure a three-dimensional figure.

figura sólida figura tridimensional.

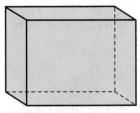

A rectangular prism is a solid figure.

©Curriculum Associates, LLC   Copying is not permitted

English	Español	Example/Ejemplo
square a quadrilateral with 4 square corners and 4 sides of equal length.	**cuadrado** cuadrilátero que tiene 4 esquinas cuadradas y 4 lados de igual longitud.	
square unit the area of a square with side lengths of 1 unit.	**unidad cuadrada** el área de un cuadrado que tiene lados de 1 unidad de longitud.	1 unit 1 unit $\{$ $\}$ 1 unit 1 unit
standard form the way a number is written with numerals.	**forma estándar** manera de escribir un número usando dígitos.	The standard form of *twelve* is 12.
subcategory a category within a larger category. It shares all the same attributes as the larger category.	**subcategoría** categoría que está dentro de otra categoría. Tiene las mismas propiedades que la categoría más amplia.	Parallelograms are a subcategory of quadrilaterals.
sum the result of addition.	**suma** el resultado de la suma.	$34 + 25 = 59$
symbol a character, such as a letter or question mark, that can be used to stand for an unknown number in an equation.	**símbolo** cualquier marca o dibujo, tal como una letra o un signo de interrogación, que puede usarse para representar un número desconocido en una ecuación.	$18 - ? = 9$

Tt

English	Español	Example/Ejemplo
tenths the parts formed when a whole is divided into 10 equal parts.	**décimos (fracciones)/ décimas (decimales)** partes que se forman cuando se divide un entero en 10 partes iguales.	
terms the numbers or shapes in a pattern.	**términos** los números o las figuras de un patrón.	3, 9, 12, 15, 18, 21, 24

©Curriculum Associates, LLC   Copying is not permitted

English	Español	Example/Ejemplo
thousandths the parts formed when a whole is divided into 1,000 equal parts.	**milésimas** partes que se forman cuando se divide un entero en 1,000 partes iguales.	$1 \div 1,000 = \frac{1}{1,000}$, or 0.001
three-dimensional solid, or having length, width, and height. For example, a cube is three-dimensional.	**tridimensional** sólido, o que tiene longitud, ancho y altura. Por ejemplo, los cubos son tridimensionales.	
trapezoid (exclusive) a quadrilateral with exactly one pair of parallel sides.	**trapecio** cuadrilátero que tiene exactamente un par de lados paralelos.	
trapezoid (inclusive) a quadrilateral with at least one pair of parallel sides.	**trapecio** cuadrilátero que tiene al menos un par de lados paralelos.	
triangle a polygon with exactly 3 sides and 3 angles.	**triángulo** polígono que tiene exactamente 3 lados y 3 ángulos.	
two-dimensional flat, or having measurement in two directions, like length and width. For example, a rectangle is two-dimensional.	**bidimensional** plano, o que tiene medidas en dos direcciones, como la longitud y el ancho. Por ejemplo, un rectángulo es bidimensional.	

©Curriculum Associates, LLC   Copying is not permitted

English	Español	Example/Ejemplo

Uu

English	Español	Example/Ejemplo
unit cube a cube with side lengths of 1 unit. A unit cube is said to have 1 cubic unit of volume, and can be used to measure the volume of a solid figure.	**cubo de unidad** cubo cuyos lados miden 1 unidad. Un cubo de unidad tiene 1 unidad cúbica de volumen y puede usarse para medir el volumen de una figura sólida.	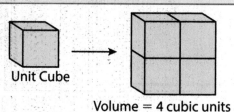 Unit Cube Volume = 4 cubic units
unit fraction a fraction with a numerator of 1. Other fractions are built from unit fractions.	**fracción unitaria** fracción cuyo numerador es 1. Otras fracciones se construyen a partir de fracciones unitarias.	$\frac{1}{4}$
unit square a square with side lengths of 1 unit. A unit square is said to have 1 square unit of area, and can be used to measure the area of a plane figure.	**cuadrado de unidad** cuadrado cuyos lados miden 1 unidad. Un cuadrado de unidad tiene 1 unidad cuadrada de área y puede usarse para medir el área de una figura plana.	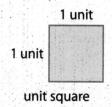 1 unit 1 unit unit square
unknown the value you need to find to solve a problem.	**desconocido** el valor que se debe hallar para resolver un problema.	$18 - ? = 9$

Vv

English	Español	Example/Ejemplo
Venn diagram a diagram that uses overlapping ovals (or other shapes) to show how sets of numbers or objects are related.	**diagrama de Venn** dibujo que contiene óvalos u otras figuras que se superponen y muestra cómo se relacionan conjuntos de números u objetos.	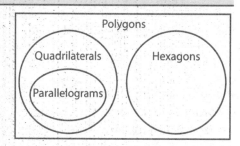 Polygons, Quadrilaterals, Hexagons, Parallelograms
vertex the point where two rays, lines, or line segments meet to form an angle.	**vértice** punto donde dos semirrectas, rectas, o segmentos de recta se unen y forman un ángulo.	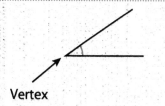 Vertex

©Curriculum Associates, LLC   Copying is not permitted

English	Español	Example/Ejemplo
volume the amount of space inside a solid figure. Volume is measured in cubic units such as cubic inches.	**volumen** cantidad de espacio que hay dentro de una figura sólida. El volumen se mide en unidades cúbicas como las pulgadas cúbicas.	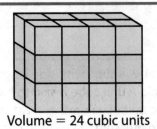 Volume = 24 cubic units

Ww

weight the measurement that tells how heavy an object is. Units of weight include ounces and pounds.	**peso** medición que dice qué tan pesado es un objeto. Las onzas y las libras son unidades de peso.	**Weight** 1 pound = 16 ounces
word form the way a number is written with words or said aloud.	**en palabras** manera en que se escribe o se dice en voz alta un número usando palabras.	467,882 four hundred sixty-seven thousand, **eight hundred eighty-two**

Xx

x-axis the horizontal number line in the coordinate plane.	**eje x** recta numérica horizontal en el plano de coordenadas.	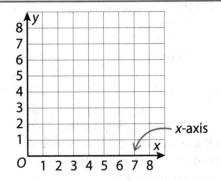
x-coordinate the first number in an ordered pair. It tells the point's horizontal distance from the origin.	**coordenada x** el primer número de un par ordenado. Indica cuál es la distancia horizontal del punto al origen.	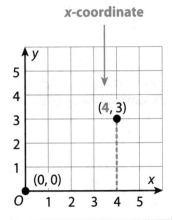

©Curriculum Associates, LLC   Copying is not permitted

English	Español	Example/Ejemplo

Yy

y-axis the vertical number line in the coordinate plane.	**eje y** recta numérica vertical en el plano de coordenadas.	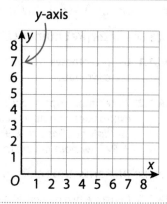
y-coordinate the second number in an ordered pair. It tells the point's vertical distance from the origin.	**coordenada y** el segundo número de un par ordenado. Indica cuál es la distancia vertical del punto al origen.	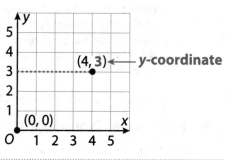
yard (yd) a unit of length in the customary system. There are 3 feet, or 36 inches, in 1 yard.	**yarda (yd)** unidad de longitud del sistema usual de Estados Unidos. 1 yarda equivale a 3 pies o a 36 pulgadas.	3 feet = 1 yard 36 inches = 1 yard

©Curriculum Associates, LLC   Copying is not permitted

Mathematics Florida Standards (MAFS) Correlations

The table below correlates each Mathematics Florida Standard (MAFS) to the Ready® Classroom Mathematics, Florida Edition lessons with comprehensive instruction on that standard.

Mathematics Florida Standards (MAFS) for Grade 5	Lessons
Operations and Algebraic Thinking	
Write and interpret numerical expressions.	
5.OA.1.1 Use parentheses, brackets, or braces in numerical expressions, and evaluate expressions with these symbols.	30
5.OA.1.2 Write simple expressions that record calculations with numbers, and interpret numerical expressions without evaluating them. *For example, express the calculation "add 8 and 7, then multiply by 2" as 2 × (8 + 7). Recognize that 3 × (18932 + 921) is three times as large as 18932 + 921, without having to calculate the indicated sum or product.*	30
Analyze patterns and relationships.	
5.OA.2.3 Generate two numerical patterns using two given rules. Identify apparent relationships between corresponding terms. Form ordered pairs consisting of corresponding terms from the two patterns, and graph the ordered pairs on a coordinate plane. *For example, given the rule "Add 3" and the starting number 0, and given the rule "Add 6" and the starting number 0, generate terms in the resulting sequences, and observe that the terms in one sequence are twice the corresponding terms in the other sequence. Explain informally why this is so.*	33
Number and Operations in Base Ten	
Understand the place value system.	
5.NBT.1.1 Recognize that in a multi-digit number, a digit in one place represents 10 times as much as it represents in the place to its right and $\frac{1}{10}$ of what it represents in the place to its left.	6
5.NBT.1.2 Explain patterns in the number of zeros of the product when multiplying a number by powers of 10, and explain patterns in the placement of the decimal point when a decimal is multiplied or divided by a power of 10. Use whole-number exponents to denote powers of 10.	7
5.NBT.1.3 Read, write, and compare decimals to thousandths.	8, 9
5.NBT.1.3a Read and write decimals to thousandths using base-ten numerals, number names, and expanded form, e.g., $347.392 = 3 \times 100 + 4 \times 10 + 7 \times 1 + 3 \times \left(\frac{1}{10}\right) + 9 \times \left(\frac{1}{100}\right) + 2 \times \left(\frac{1}{1000}\right)$.	8
5.NF.1.3b Compare two decimals to thousandths based on meanings of the digits in each place, using >, =, and < symbols to record the results of comparisons.	9
5.NBT.1.4 Use place value understanding to round decimals to any place.	9

The Mathematical Practice standards are integrated throughout the lessons.
Mathematics Florida Standards (MAFS) ©2014. Florida Department of Education.

©Curriculum Associates, LLC   Copying is not permitted.

Number and Operations in Base Ten *continued*

Perform operations with multi-digit whole numbers and with decimals to hundredths.

	Lessons
5.NBT.2.5 Fluently multiply multi-digit whole numbers using the standard algorithm.	4
5.NBT.2.6 Find whole-number quotients of whole numbers with up to four-digit dividends and two-digit divisors, using strategies based on place value, the properties of operations, and/or the relationship between multiplication and division. Illustrate and explain the calculation by using equations, rectangular arrays, and/or area models.	5
5.NBT.2.7 Add, subtract, multiply, and divide decimals to hundredths, using concrete models or drawings and strategies based on place value, properties of operations, and/or the relationship between addition and subtraction; relate the strategy to a written method and explain the reasoning used.	10, 11, 14, 15, 16, 17

Number and Operations—Fractions

Use equivalent fractions as a strategy to add and subtract fractions.

	Lessons
5.NF.1.1 Add and subtract fractions with unlike denominators (including mixed numbers) by replacing given fractions with equivalent fractions in such a way as to produce an equivalent sum or difference of fractions with like denominators. *For example, $\frac{2}{3} + \frac{5}{4} = \frac{8}{12} + \frac{15}{12} = \frac{23}{12}$.* (*In general, $\frac{a}{b} + \frac{c}{d} = \frac{(ad + bc)}{bd}$.*)	12, 13
5.NF.1.2 Solve word problems involving addition and subtraction of fractions referring to the same whole, including cases of unlike denominators, e.g., by using visual fraction models or equations to represent the problem. Use benchmark fractions and number sense of fractions to estimate mentally and assess the reasonableness of answers. *For example, recognize an incorrect result $\frac{2}{5} + \frac{1}{2} = \frac{3}{7}$, by observing that $\frac{3}{7} < \frac{1}{2}$.*	12, 13, 14

Apply and extend previous understandings of multiplication and division to multiply and divide fractions.

	Lessons
5.NF.2.3 Interpret a fraction as division of the numerator by the denominator $\left(\frac{a}{b} = a \div b\right)$. Solve word problems involving division of whole numbers leading to answers in the form of fractions or mixed numbers, e.g., by using visual fraction models or equations to represent the problem. *For example, interpret $\frac{3}{4}$ as the result of dividing 3 by 4, noting that $\frac{3}{4}$ multiplied by 4 equals 3, and that when 3 wholes are shared equally among 4 people each person has a share of size $\frac{3}{4}$. If 9 people want to share a 50-pound sack of rice equally by weight, how many pounds of rice should each person get? Between what two whole numbers does your answer lie?*	18
5.NF.2.4 Apply and extend previous understandings of multiplication to multiply a fraction or whole number by a fraction.	19, 20
5.NF.2.4a Interpret the product $\left(\frac{a}{b}\right) \times q$ as a parts of a partition of q into b equal parts; equivalently, as the result of a sequence of operations $a \times q \div b$. *For example, use a visual fraction model to show $\left(\frac{2}{3}\right) \times 4 = \frac{8}{3}$, and create a story context for this equation. Do the same with $\left(\frac{2}{3}\right) \times \left(\frac{4}{5}\right) = \frac{8}{15}$. (In general, $\left(\frac{a}{b}\right) \times \left(\frac{c}{d}\right) = \frac{ac}{bd}$.)*	19

The Mathematical Practice standards are integrated throughout the lessons.

©Curriculum Associates, LLC   Copying is not permitted.

Number and Operations—Fractions *continued*

Apply and extend previous understandings of multiplication and division to multiply and divide fractions.

	Lessons
5.NF.2.4b Find the area of a rectangle with fractional side lengths by tiling it with unit squares of the appropriate unit fraction side lengths, and show that the area is the same as would be found by multiplying the side lengths. Multiply fractional side lengths to find areas of rectangles, and represent fraction products as rectangular areas.	20
5.NF.2.5 Interpret multiplication as scaling (resizing), by:	21
5.NF.2.5a Comparing the size of a product to the size of one factor on the basis of the size of the other factor, without performing the indicated multiplication.	21
5.NF.2.5b Explaining why multiplying a given number by a fraction greater than 1 results in a product greater than the given number (recognizing multiplication by whole numbers greater than 1 as a familiar case); explaining why multiplying a given number by a fraction less than 1 results in a product smaller than the given number; and relating the principle of fraction equivalence $\frac{a}{b} = \frac{(n \times a)}{(n \times b)}$ to the effect of multiplying $\frac{a}{b}$ by 1.	21
5.NF.2.6 Solve real world problems involving multiplication of fractions and mixed numbers, e.g., by using visual fraction models or equations to represent the problem.	22
5.NF.2.7 Apply and extend previous understandings of division to divide unit fractions by whole numbers and whole numbers by unit fractions.	23, 24
5.NF.2.7a Interpret division of a unit fraction by a non-zero whole number, and compute such quotients. *For example, create a story context for $\left(\frac{1}{3}\right) \div 4$, and use a visual fraction model to show the quotient. Use the relationship between multiplication and division to explain that $\left(\frac{1}{3}\right) \div 4 = \frac{1}{12}$ because $\left(\frac{1}{12}\right) \times 4 = \frac{1}{3}$.*	23
5.NF.2.7b Interpret division of a whole number by a unit fraction, and compute such quotients. *For example, create a story context for $4 \div \left(\frac{1}{5}\right)$, and use a visual fraction model to show the quotient. Use the relationship between multiplication and division to explain that $4 \div \left(\frac{1}{5}\right) = 20$ because $20 \times \left(\frac{1}{5}\right) = 4$.*	23
5.NF.2.7c Solve real world problems involving division of unit fractions by non-zero whole numbers and division of whole numbers by unit fractions, e.g., by using visual fraction models and equations to represent the problem. *For example, how much chocolate will each person get if 3 people share $\frac{1}{2}$ lb of chocolate equally? How many $\frac{1}{3}$-cup servings are in 2 cups of raisins?*	24

Measurement and Data

Convert like measurement units within a given measurement system.

	Lessons
5.MD.1.1 Convert among different-sized standard measurement units (i.e., km, m, cm; kg, g; lb, oz.; l, ml; hr, min, sec) within a given measurement system (e.g., convert 5 cm to 0.05 m), and use these conversions in solving multi-step, real world problems.	25, 26

The Mathematical Practice standards are integrated throughout the lessons.

©Curriculum Associates, LLC   Copying is not permitted.

Measurement and Data *continued*

Represent and interpret data.

5.MD.2.2 Make a line plot to display a data set of measurements in fractions of a unit $\left(\frac{1}{2}, \frac{1}{4}, \frac{1}{8}\right)$. Use operations on fractions for this grade to solve problems involving information presented in line plots. *For example, given different measurements of liquid in identical beakers, find the amount of liquid each beaker would contain if the total amount in all the beakers were redistributed equally.*	27

Geometric measurement: understand concepts of volume and relate volume to multiplication and to addition.

5.MD.3.3 Recognize volume as an attribute of solid figures and understand concepts of volume measurement.	1
5.MD.3.3a A cube with side length 1 unit, called a "unit cube," is said to have "one cubic unit" of volume, and can be used to measure volume.	1
5.MD.3.3b A solid figure which can be packed without gaps or overlaps using *n* unit cubes is said to have a volume of *n* cubic units.	1
5.MD.3.4 Measure volumes by counting unit cubes, using cubic cm, cubic in, cubic ft, and improvised units.	2
5.MD.3.5 Relate volume to the operations of multiplication and addition and solve real world and mathematical problems involving volume.	2, 3
5.MD.3.5a Find the volume of a right rectangular prism with whole-number side lengths by packing it with unit cubes, and show that the volume is the same as would be found by multiplying the edge lengths, equivalently by multiplying the height by the area of the base. Represent threefold whole-number products as volumes, e.g., to represent the associative property of multiplication.	2, 3
5.MD.3.5b Apply the formulas $V = l \times w \times h$ and $V = B \times h$ for rectangular prisms to find volumes of right rectangular prisms with whole-number edge lengths in the context of solving real world and mathematical problems.	3
5.MD.3.5c Recognize volume as additive. Find volumes of solid figures composed of two non-overlapping right rectangular prisms by adding the volumes of the non-overlapping parts, applying this technique to solve real world problems.	3

Geometry

Graph points on the coordinate plane to solve real-world and mathematical problems.

5.G.1.1 Use a pair of perpendicular number lines, called axes, to define a coordinate system, with the intersection of the lines (the origin) arranged to coincide with the 0 on each line and a given point in the plane located by using an ordered pair of numbers, called its coordinates. Understand that the first number indicates how far to travel from the origin in the direction of one axis, and the second number indicates how far to travel in the direction of the second axis, with the convention that the names of the two axes and the coordinates correspond (e.g., *x*-axis and *x*-coordinate, *y*-axis and *y*-coordinate).	31

The Mathematical Practice standards are integrated throughout the lessons.

©Curriculum Associates, LLC   Copying is not permitted.

Geometry *continued*

Graph points on the coordinate plane to solve real-world and mathematical problems. *continued*

5.G.1.2	Represent real world and mathematical problems by graphing points in the first quadrant of the coordinate plane, and interpret coordinate values of points in the context of the situation.	32

Classify two-dimensional figures into categories based on their properties.

5.G.2.3	Understand that attributes belonging to a category of two-dimensional figures also belong to all subcategories of that category. *For example, all rectangles have four right angles and squares are rectangles, so all squares have four right angles.*	28
5.G.2.4	Classify and organize two-dimensional figures into Venn diagrams based on the attributes of the figures.	29

The Mathematical Practice standards are integrated throughout the lessons.

©Curriculum Associates, LLC   Copying is not permitted.

Understanding of Volume

Name: _____

1 Write an addition equation to find the volume of the prism.

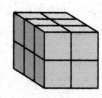

1 unit cube

Write a multiplication equation to find the volume of the prism.

The volume is _____ cubic units.

2 Write an addition equation to find the volume of the prism.

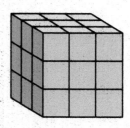

1 unit cube

Write a multiplication equation to find the volume of the prism.

The volume is _____ cubic units.

3 Write an addition equation to find the volume of the prism.

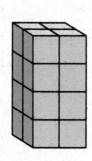

1 unit cube

Write a multiplication equation to find the volume of the prism.

The volume is _____ cubic units.

4 Write an addition equation to find the volume of the prism.

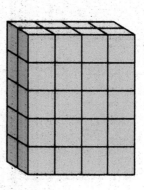

Write a multiplication equation to find the volume of the prism.

1 unit cube

The volume is _____ cubic units.

5 Which method do you like best? Explain why.

©Curriculum Associates, LLC   Copying is not permitted   Use with Lesson 1   **A33**

Finding Volume Using Unit Cubes

Name: _____

Write an addition equation and a multiplication equation to find the volume of each rectangular prism.

1

2 ft
2 ft   4 ft

Addition: _____

Multiplication: _____

Volume: _____

2

2 cm
4 cm   3 cm

Addition: _____

Multiplication: _____

Volume: _____

3

4 in.
1 in.   2 in.

Addition: _____

Multiplication: _____

Volume: _____

4

3 ft
2 ft   2 ft

Addition: _____

Multiplication: _____

Volume: _____

5

3 cm
2 cm   3 cm

Addition: _____

Multiplication: _____

Volume: _____

6

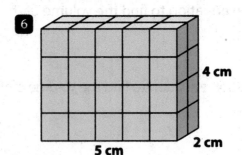

4 cm
5 cm   2 cm

Addition: _____

Multiplication: _____

Volume: _____

©Curriculum Associates, LLC   Copying is not permitted

Finding Volume Using Unit Cubes *continued*

Name: _____

7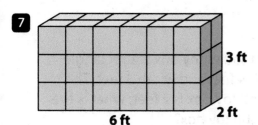

3 ft

6 ft   2 ft

Addition: _____

Multiplication: _____

Volume: _____

8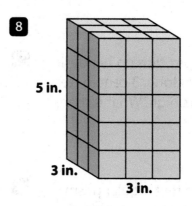

5 in.

3 in.

3 in.

Addition: _____

Multiplication: _____

Volume: _____

9 A box has a volume of 32 cubic inches. What could be the length, the width, and the height of the box? How could you pack unit cubes into the box to prove your answer is correct?

Finding Volume Using Formulas

Name: _____

Solve each problem.

1 Susan has a box for paper clips on her desk. The box is 6 centimeters long, 3 centimeters wide, and 2 centimeters high. What is the volume of the box?

2 The base of Jada's toy box is a rectangle with length 4 feet and width 3 feet. The height of the toy box is 2 feet. What is the volume of the toy box?

3 What is the volume of a rectangular prism with a length of 4 centimeters, a width of 1 centimeter, and a height of 7 centimeters?

4 How much space is taken up by a rectangular tissue box that is 5 inches long, 4 inches wide, and 5 inches high?

5 The base of Tim's closet is a rectangle that is 4 feet long and 2 feet wide. The closet is 7 feet high. What is the volume of Tim's closet?

6 A rectangular prism is 3 inches high, 9 inches long, and 3 inches wide. What is the volume of the prism?

7 The base of a rectangular prism is 5 meters long and 8 meters wide. Its height is 3 meters. What is the volume of the prism?

8 A recipe box is 6 inches long, 3 inches wide, and 4 inches high. What is the volume of the recipe box?

9 Esteban buys cereal in a box that is 10 inches high, 7 inches long, and 2 inches wide. What is the volume of the cereal box?

10 The base of a rectangular crayon box is 8 centimeters long and 4 centimeters wide. Its height is 10 centimeters. What is the volume of the crayon box?

11 What volume formula did you use to solve problem 10? Explain how you used the formula.

©Curriculum Associates, LLC   Copying is not permitted

Breaking Apart Figures to Find Volume

Name: _____

What is the volume of the solid figure?

1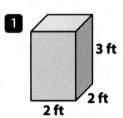
3 ft
2 ft
2 ft

_____

2
3 ft
2 ft
6 ft

_____

3
3 ft
2 ft
2 ft
4 ft
2 ft

_____

4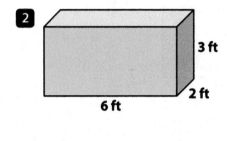
2 cm
5 cm
7 cm
2 cm
8 cm

_____

5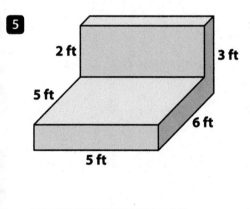
2 ft
3 ft
5 ft
6 ft
5 ft

_____

6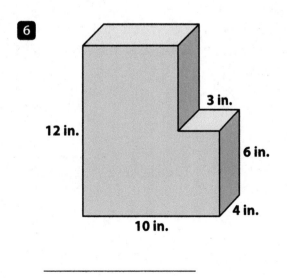
3 in.
12 in.
6 in.
4 in.
10 in.

_____

**Breaking Apart Figures
to Find Volume** *continued*

Name: _____

7

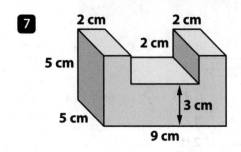

_____

8

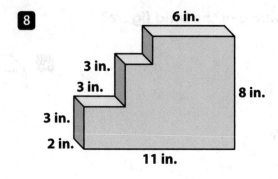

_____

9 What are two different ways to break apart the figure in problem 3 to find its volume?

©Curriculum Associates, LLC   Copying is not permitted

Multiplying Multi-Digit Whole Numbers

Name: _____

Estimate. Circle all the problems with products between 3,000 and 9,000. Then find the exact products of only the problems you circled.

1   132
      × 34

2   247
      × 15

3   145
      × 23

4   308
      × 12

5   158
      × 41

6   364
      × 32

7   400
      × 29

8   254
      × 17

9   187
      × 42

10   216
      × 12

11   323
      × 18

12   194
      × 26

13   317
      × 14

14   385
      × 31

15   285
      × 27

16 What strategies did you use to solve the problems? Explain.

©Curriculum Associates, LLC   Copying is not permitted

Multiplying with the Standard Algorithm

Name: _____

The answers are mixed up at the bottom of the page. Cross out the answers as you complete the problems.

1
```
   580
×   30
```

2
```
 3,104
×    18
```

3
```
 1,482
×    38
```

4
```
 1,085
×    17
```

5
```
 1,236
×    55
```

6
```
 1,625
×    18
```

7
```
 2,105
×    13
```

8
```
 1,788
×    15
```

9
```
 2,500
×    19
```

10
```
   648
×   32
```

11
```
 2,409
×    23
```

12
```
   306
×   62
```

13
```
 2,417
×    24
```

14
```
   650
×   35
```

15
```
   962
×    44
```

Answers

20,736	17,400	27,365	47,500	55,872
18,972	18,445	26,820	67,980	56,316
22,750	29,250	55,407	42,328	58,008

©Curriculum Associates, LLC   Copying is not permitted

Estimating Quotients

Name: _____

Estimate each quotient.

1 250 ÷ 52

_____

2 2,500 ÷ 52

_____

3 82 ÷ 41

_____

4 802 ÷ 41

_____

5 8,002 ÷ 41

_____

6 789 ÷ 81

_____

7 3,210 ÷ 78

_____

8 6,912 ÷ 11

_____

9 2,750 ÷ 28

_____

10 5,675 ÷ 73

_____

11 4,915 ÷ 69

_____

12 6,205 ÷ 32

_____

13 8,955 ÷ 29

_____

14 4,140 ÷ 18

_____

15 7,998 ÷ 91

_____

16 Estimate 752 ÷ 17. What strategy did you use to solve the problem? Explain.

17 Estimate 1,450 ÷ 24. What strategy did you use to solve the problem? Explain.

©Curriculum Associates, LLC   Copying is not permitted

Using Estimation and Area Models to Divide

Name: _____

Check each answer by multiplying the divisor by the quotient. If the answer is incorrect, cross out the answer and write the correct answer.

Division Problems	Student Answers	
1 516 ÷ 12	~~48~~ 43	Check: 12 × 48 = 576
2 837 ÷ 31	27	
3 351 ÷ 13	57	
4 918 ÷ 54	22	
5 896 ÷ 32	23	
6 1,482 ÷ 78	14	
7 1,012 ÷ 11	82	
8 1,344 ÷ 56	24	

9 Explain how you could know that the answers to two of the problems are incorrect without multiplying.

©Curriculum Associates, LLC   Copying is not permitted

Using Area Models and Partial Quotients to Divide

Name: _____

**Estimate. Circle all the problems that will have quotients greater than 30.
Then find the exact quotients of only the problems you circled.**

1 540 ÷ 12

_____

2 798 ÷ 38

_____

3 429 ÷ 11

_____

4 931 ÷ 19

_____

5 925 ÷ 25

_____

6 390 ÷ 15

_____

7 1,071 ÷ 51

_____

8 1,326 ÷ 13

_____

9 1,856 ÷ 32

_____

10 2,952 ÷ 72

_____

11 1,869 ÷ 89

_____

12 1,798 ÷ 29

_____

13 Select a problem you did not circle. Describe two different ways you could use estimation to tell the quotient is not greater than 30.

©Curriculum Associates, LLC   Copying is not permitted

Understanding of Place Value

Name: _____

1 The decimal grid in each model represents 1 whole. Shade each model to show the decimal number below the model.

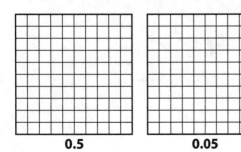

0.5   **0.05**

Complete the comparison statements.

0.05 is _____ of 0.5.   0.5 is _____ times the value of 0.05.

Complete the equations.

0.5 ÷ _____ = 0.05   0.05 × _____ = 0.5

2 Draw a number line from 0 to 2. Then draw and label points at 2 and 0.2.

←————————————————————————→

Use the number line to explain why 2 is 10 times the value of 0.2.

Complete the equations to show the relationship between 2 and 0.2.

0.2 × _____ = 2

2 ÷ _____ = 0.2

3 Which type of model do you like best? Explain why.

          ©Curriculum Associates, LLC   Copying is not permitted

Fluency and Skills Practice

Understanding Powers of 10

Name: _____

Multiply or divide.

1 $6 \div 10$

_____

2 $0.6 \div 10$

_____

3 $6 \div 10^2$

_____

4 $0.6 \div 10^2$

_____

5 $6 \div 10^3$

_____

6 $60 \div 10^3$

_____

7 0.3×10

_____

8 0.3×10^2

_____

9 0.3×10^3

_____

10 0.03×10^2

_____

11 0.003×10^2

_____

12 0.03×10^3

_____

13 $72 \div 10$

_____

14 0.72×10^2

_____

15 $7{,}200 \div 10^3$

_____

16 $20 \div 10^2$

_____

17 0.9×10^3

_____

18 0.001×10^2

_____

19 $54 \div 10$

_____

20 $150 \div 10^3$

_____

21 0.46×10^3

_____

22 What strategies did you use to solve the problems? Explain.

©Curriculum Associates, LLC   Copying is not permitted

Reading a Decimal in Word Form

Name: _____

What is the word form of each decimal?

1 0.2

_____

2 0.02

_____

3 0.002

_____

4 0.12

_____

5 0.012

_____

6 0.102

_____

7 1.002

_____

8 9.4

_____

9 90.04

_____

10 0.94

_____

11 500.2

_____

12 8.008

_____

13 700.06

_____

14 6.335

_____

15 3,000.001

_____

16 What strategies did you use to help you read the decimals? Explain.

©Curriculum Associates, LLC Copying is not permitted

Writing a Decimal in Standard Form

Name: _____

What decimal represents each number?

1 one and six tenths

_____

2 eight and eleven hundredths

_____

3 $6 \times 1 + 5 \times \frac{1}{10}$

_____

4 thirteen and thirteen thousandths

_____

5 $2 \times 10 + 7 \times \frac{1}{10} + 3 \times \frac{1}{100}$

_____

6 $4 \times 1 + 1 \times \frac{1}{100} + 9 \times \frac{1}{1,000}$

_____

7 five hundred twelve thousandths

_____

8 $8 \times 100 + 2 \times \frac{1}{10} + 8 \times \frac{1}{1,000}$

_____

9 $2 \times 1 + 4 \times \frac{1}{100}$

_____

10 forty-two and forty-one hundredths

_____

11 $7 \times 100 + 2 \times 10 + 3 \times 1 + 6 \times \frac{1}{10}$

_____

12 twelve and sixty-eight thousandths

_____

13 $3 \times 1,000 + 6 \times 100 + 3 \times 10 + 7 \times \frac{1}{10} + 2 \times \frac{1}{100} + 8 \times \frac{1}{1,000}$

_____

14 nine hundred fifty-six and four hundred twenty-seven thousandths

_____

15 How was writing decimals for numbers in word form different from writing decimals for numbers in expanded form?

Comparing Decimals

Name: _____

Write the symbol <, =, or > in each comparison statement.

1 0.02 ◯ 0.002

2 0.05 ◯ 0.5

3 0.74 ◯ 0.84

4 0.74 ◯ 0.084

5 1.2 ◯ 1.25

6 5.130 ◯ 5.13

7 3.201 ◯ 3.099

8 0.159 ◯ 1.590

9 8.269 ◯ 8.268

10 4.60 ◯ 4.060

11 302.026 ◯ 300.226

12 0.237 ◯ 0.223

13 3.033 ◯ 3.303

14 9.074 ◯ 9.47

15 6.129 ◯ 6.19

16 567.45 ◯ 564.75

17 78.967 ◯ 78.957

18 5.346 ◯ 5.4

19 12.112 ◯ 12.121

20 26.2 ◯ 26.200

21 100.32 ◯ 100.232

22 What strategies did you use to solve the problems? Explain.

©Curriculum Associates, LLC   Copying is not permitted

Rounding Decimals

Name: _____

Round each decimal to the nearest tenth.

1 0.32

_____

2 3.87

_____

3 0.709

_____

4 12.75

_____

5 12.745

_____

6 645.059

_____

Round each decimal to the nearest hundredth.

7 1.079

_____

8 0.854

_____

9 0.709

_____

10 12.745

_____

11 645.059

_____

12 50.501

_____

Round each decimal to the nearest whole number.

13 1.47

_____

14 12.5

_____

15 200.051

_____

16 Write two different decimals that are the same value when rounded to the nearest tenth. Explain why the rounded values are the same.

17 Round 1.299 to the nearest tenth and to the nearest hundredth. Explain why the rounded values are equivalent.

Adding Decimals

Name: _____

Circle all the problems with sums less than 5.
Then find the exact sums of only the problems you circled.

1 0.24 + 4.25

_____

2 4.8 + 0.16

_____

3 2.31 + 2.075

_____

4 2.31 + 2.7

_____

5 0.909 + 4.09

_____

6 3.99 + 1.109

_____

7 2.675 + 2.325

_____

8 3.775 + 0.225

_____

9 2.06 + 2.933

_____

10 2.6 + 2.933

_____

11 1.809 + 3.091

_____

12 3.01 + 1.991

_____

13 1.83 + 3.1 + 0.1

_____

14 0.012 + 3.79 + 1.101

_____

15 2.6 + 2.04 + 0.099

_____

16 What strategies did you use to solve the problems?

©Curriculum Associates, LLC Copying is not permitted

Subtracting Decimals to Hundredths

Name: _____

The answers are mixed up at the bottom of the page. Cross out the answers as you complete the problems.

1 7.5 − 1.2

_____

2 10.75 − 4.13

_____

3 20.2 − 14.8

_____

4 6.12 − 0.7

_____

5 41.5 − 33.25

_____

6 15.9 − 8.92

_____

7 105.53 − 99.28

_____

8 9.46 − 3.68

_____

9 74 − 65.9

_____

10 5.05 − 0.56

_____

11 31.27 − 23.67

_____

12 256.4 − 248.38

_____

13 12 − 4.39

_____

14 1,280.01 − 1,272.77

_____

15 500.2 − 494.94

_____

Answers

6.25	5.26	6.62	8.1	7.6
4.49	8.25	7.61	6.98	5.42
7.24	5.4	8.02	5.78	6.3

©Curriculum Associates, LLC   Copying is not permitted

Adding On to Subtract

Name: _____

Add on to subtract.

1 10.00 − 9.99

_____

2 10.00 − 8.99

_____

3 10.00 − 8.75

_____

4 5.10 − 4.75

_____

5 5.10 − 3.75

_____

6 5.10 − 3.56

_____

7 18.2 − 14.85

_____

8 62.25 − 59.74

_____

9 32.2 − 27.39

_____

10 18.01 − 13.07

_____

11 150.35 − 147.9

_____

12 95.2 − 68.67

_____

13 How did you solve problem 7 by adding on? Describe each step.

14 Do you think adding on would be a good strategy to solve 5.98 − 1.11? Explain your reasoning.

©Curriculum Associates, LLC   Copying is not permitted

Fluency and Skills Practice

Adding Fractions with Unlike Denominators

Name: _____

Add.

1 $\frac{1}{2} + \frac{1}{4}$

_____

2 $\frac{1}{2} + \frac{3}{8}$

_____

3 $\frac{1}{2} + \frac{1}{3}$

_____

4 $\frac{1}{3} + \frac{1}{4}$

_____

5 $\frac{5}{6} + \frac{1}{12}$

_____

6 $\frac{1}{3} + \frac{2}{5}$

_____

7 $\frac{5}{6} + \frac{2}{3}$

_____

8 $\frac{3}{4} + \frac{5}{6}$

_____

9 $\frac{7}{9} + \frac{1}{6}$

_____

10 $\frac{7}{8} + \frac{2}{3}$

_____

11 $\frac{3}{2} + \frac{3}{5}$

_____

12 $\frac{9}{8} + \frac{5}{6}$

_____

13 What is a different common denominator you could use in problem 2? Describe how you would add the fractions using this different common denominator. Is the result equivalent to the sum found in problem 2?

Adding with Mixed Numbers

Name: _____

Add.

1 $4\frac{7}{8} + \frac{1}{8}$

2 $4\frac{7}{8} + \frac{1}{4}$

3 $4\frac{7}{8} + \frac{1}{2}$

_____

_____

_____

4 $2\frac{3}{4} + \frac{1}{3}$

5 $2\frac{3}{4} + \frac{2}{3}$

6 $2\frac{3}{4} + \frac{5}{6}$

_____

_____

_____

7 $1\frac{2}{5} + 1\frac{1}{2}$

8 $2\frac{4}{5} + 3\frac{1}{2}$

9 $3\frac{2}{3} + 3\frac{2}{5}$

_____

_____

_____

10 $4\frac{5}{8} + 2\frac{2}{3}$

11 $5\frac{3}{4} + 2\frac{3}{5}$

12 $3\frac{5}{6} + 2\frac{7}{8}$

_____

_____

_____

13 What strategy did you use to solve problem 3? Describe each step.

©Curriculum Associates, LLC Copying is not permitted

Fluency and Skills Practice

Subtracting Fractions with Unlike Denominators

Name: _____

Subtract.

1 $\frac{1}{2} - \frac{1}{4}$

_____

2 $\frac{1}{2} - \frac{3}{8}$

_____

3 $\frac{1}{2} - \frac{1}{3}$

_____

4 $\frac{1}{3} - \frac{1}{4}$

_____

5 $\frac{5}{6} - \frac{5}{12}$

_____

6 $\frac{3}{4} - \frac{1}{6}$

_____

7 $\frac{7}{8} - \frac{3}{4}$

_____

8 $\frac{1}{2} - \frac{2}{5}$

_____

9 $\frac{3}{4} - \frac{3}{5}$

_____

10 $\frac{2}{3} - \frac{3}{5}$

_____

11 $\frac{5}{6} - \frac{3}{8}$

_____

12 $\frac{7}{8} - \frac{2}{3}$

_____

13 How could you check your work in problem 4? Describe each step.

©Curriculum Associates, LLC   Copying is not permitted

Subtracting with Mixed Numbers

Name: _____

Subtract.

1 $2\frac{1}{8} - \frac{1}{4}$

_____

2 $2\frac{1}{8} - \frac{1}{2}$

_____

3 $2\frac{1}{8} - \frac{3}{4}$

_____

4 $2\frac{1}{2} - \frac{2}{3}$

_____

5 $2\frac{1}{4} - 1\frac{1}{3}$

_____

6 $3\frac{1}{6} - 1\frac{3}{4}$

_____

7 $7\frac{2}{5} - 3\frac{1}{2}$

_____

8 $5\frac{3}{8} - 4\frac{1}{6}$

_____

9 $8\frac{2}{3} - 3\frac{4}{5}$

_____

10 $6\frac{2}{5} - 3\frac{3}{4}$

_____

11 $9\frac{3}{8} - 3\frac{2}{3}$

_____

12 $14\frac{1}{8} - 9\frac{5}{6}$

_____

13 What pattern did you notice in problems 1 through 3? Explain how this helped you subtract.

©Curriculum Associates, LLC   Copying is not permitted

Estimating in Word Problems with Fractions

Name: _____

Solve the problems. Estimate to tell if your solution is reasonable. Show your work.

1 Jim mails one package that weighs $\frac{3}{8}$ pound and another that weighs $\frac{2}{3}$ pound. What is the total weight of both packages?

2 Rosa needs $5\frac{1}{4}$ yards of ribbon for a craft project. She already has $2\frac{7}{8}$ yards of ribbon. How many more yards of ribbon does she need to buy?

3 To make fruit punch, Tyrone needs $3\frac{3}{8}$ quarts of orange juice and $3\frac{3}{4}$ quarts of cranberry juice. How many quarts of juice does he need in all?

©Curriculum Associates, LLC   Copying is not permitted

**Estimating in Word Problems
with Fractions** *continued*

Name: _____

4 Lin spent $\frac{5}{6}$ hour on math homework and $1\frac{5}{8}$ hours on science homework. How many hours in all did she spend on homework for both subjects?

5 Sandra rode her bike $9\frac{1}{3}$ miles on Monday and $6\frac{4}{5}$ miles on Tuesday. How many more miles did she ride on Monday than on Tuesday?

6 How can you make a high estimate for the sum of two fractions in a word problem?

   ©Curriculum Associates, LLC   Copying is not permitted

Using Estimation with Decimals

Name: _____

Solve the problems.

1 Lori needs at least 12 liters of water to fill a water cooler. She has a container with 4.55 liters of water, a container with 3.25 liters of water, and a container with 4.85 liters of water. Does she have enough water? Use estimation only to decide. Explain why you are confident in your estimate.

2 Nia wants the total weight of her luggage to be no more than 100 pounds. She has three suitcases that weigh 30.8 pounds, 35.42 pounds, and 33.28 pounds. Is the total weight within the limit? Use only estimation to decide. Explain how you know your estimate gives you the correct answer.

3 Omar measures one machine part with length 4.392 inches and another part with length 6.82 inches. What is the difference in length? Use estimation to check your answer for reasonableness.

Using Estimation with Decimals *continued*

Name: _____

4 Kyle wants to buy a hat for $5.75, a T-shirt for $7.65, and a keychain for $3.15. He has $16. Does he have enough money? Use estimation only to decide. Explain why you are confident in your estimate.

5 For his hiking club, Ricardo is making a container of trail mix with 3.5 kilograms of nuts. He has 1.78 kilograms of peanuts and 0.625 kilogram of almonds. The rest of the nuts will be cashews. How many kilograms of cashews does he need? Use estimation to check your answer for reasonableness.

6 Suppose you want to be sure that the total cost of three items does not go over a certain amount. How can you only use estimation to solve the problem?

©Curriculum Associates, LLC   Copying is not permitted

Acknowledgments

Front Cover Credits

©Paul Bradbury/OJO Images/Getty Images

Photography Credits

United States coin images (unless otherwise indicated) from the United States Mint.
Images used under license from **Shutterstock.com**.

iii ArtMari, freedomnaruk; **iv** graphicmaker, PrimaStockPhoto; **v** timquo; **vi** Danielle Balderas, Istimages; **vii** Aila Images, Cartarium, jeep5d; **HBi** ArtMari, Rawpixel.com, Pixfiction, Disavorabuth; **HB1** Africa Studio, opicobello; **HB2** iadams; **HB3** Palabra; **HB5** Harvepino; **HB6** Tatiana Popova; **HB8** Chiyacat; **HB9** Kyselova Inna, Markus Mainka; **HB10** ArtMari; **HB11** Disavorabuth; **HB12** ArtMari, Disavorabuth; **HB13–HB14** ArtMari; **HB16** Rawpixel.com; **1** iavizzara, Peter Turner Photography; **8** Quang Ho; **9** Yuguesh Fagoonee; **14** FabrikaSimf; **17** Issarawat Tattong, Zora Avagyan; **20** Y Photo Studio; **22** Mega Pixel; **23** Picsfive; **32** c12, Chaowat S; **36** Africa Studio, heraldmuc; **37** Sergey Sklezney, Tibet Saisema; **38** 5 second Studio, Lubava; **39** Nadiia Korol; **40** Garsya; **41** HeinzTeh; **42** Stephen Rees; **43** Kitch Bain, M. Unal Ozmen, Patty Chan; **44** Nik Merkulov; **46** Beth Swanson; **54** Gruffi, Inc., ORLIO; **58** ananaline; **59** Mehmet Cetin, Inc., Olga Popova; **60** Ievgenii Meyer; **62** Creativestockexchange; **64** Ivan Kurmyshov; **68** Qwasder1987; **72** PhotoStock10; **73** Mathier; **76** Cory Thoman, Studiovin; **77** Konstantin Faraktinov; **80** Aluna1, Nerthuz; **81** sumire8; **82** freedomnaruk, Natasha Pankina; **84** kibri_ho; **86** Dr Ajay Kumar Singh, Liskus, Roblan; **87** Nertuz; **88** Nerthuz, Topform; **91** Lucie Lang; **93** Trong Nguyen; **94** Nares Soumsomboon; **96** Sharon Day; **98** Photka; **100** Steve Collender; **101** Evgeny Karandaev, Natasha Pankina; **102** Kleber Cordeiro, Natasha Pankina; **103** Africa Studio, Cory Thoman **104** vitec; **106** Bernatskaya, Vitec; **108** Natasha Pankina, Worker; **110** Sanit Fuangnakhon; **111** Tatevosian Yana; **117** Bubutu; **130** Irin-K, windu; **131** Capslock, rCarner; **132** Elnur, Rica Photography; **137** rCarnder; **148** Africa Studio, Stefano T; **149** Edward Hardam, Photogal; **150** Masterchief_Productions; **155** Bezikus, mhatzapa; **156** PrimaStockPhoto; **160** Iuliia Timofeeva; **163** GrashAlex; **166** Ajt, jingdi, Odua Images; **167** Garsya, Pavel L Photo and Video; **170** Artmim; **171** neotemlpars; **172** pio3; **174** Eric Isselee; **175** Quang Ho; **176** Eric Isselee; **177** Jojje; **180** Julian Rovagnati; **181** 6493866629; **182–183** Yellow Cat; **185** Somboon Bunproy; **188** Africa Studio, Krasowit, Ostancov Vladislav; **189** Pete Saloutos; **190** Mny-Jhee; **192** Dmitriy Halacevich; **193** Craig Barhorst, Stockagogo; **194** Jojoo4; **196** Goran Bogicevic; **197** Andrey_Popov; **198** irin-k; **199** AVprophoto; **200** Ruslan Semichev; **204** Eric Isselee, r. classen; **205** FotoRequest, Sari Oneal; **206** Mike Truchon; **208** 3DMAVR; **209** Hue Ta; **210** Hong Vo; **214** fivespots; **218** inxti; **219** Maks Narodenko; **220** Y Photo Studio; **222** Moving Moment; **223** Vitaly Raduntsev; **226** 1989studio, jiangdi, LAURA_VA, MaraZe; **227** Art65395; **228** Anastasia Prisunko; **230** HomeStudio; **231** Givaga; **232** Anna Kucherova; **236** Africa Studio; **237** Eivaisla; **240** JeniFoto; **242** gresei; **244** Imfoto; **245** Your Design; **246** Baibaz; **247** MIGUEL GARCIA SAAVEDRA; **248** graphicmaker, pirtuss; **249** Kostsov; **250** Tish1; **252** Valzan; **253** Mariyana M; **255** Kiprej, kubais, Mariyana M; **256** Lunaticm; **258** artjazz, mhatzapa; **259** Nungning20; **260** 3DMAVR, serazetdinov; **266** Ayman alakhras, Mega Pixel, Natasha Pankina; **267** Perun; **269** paulista; **270** Sirtravelalot, Tapui, Valzan; **271** Elena Zajchikova, Wk1003mike; **272** Galushko Sergey; **274** Grey_and; **275** Alisafarov; **276** Ryzhkov Photography; **278** art'n'lera, Tim Masters; **280** George3973, Marionhassold, Rtstudio; **281** DenisNata; **282** DenisNata, mhatzapa, urfin; **284** marilyn barbone; **286** JeniFoto; **288** Victor Moussa; **289** liskus, oksana2010; **290** Picsfive; **291** Crepesoles, Natasha Pankina; **292** Natasha Pankina, Susan Schmitz; **294–295** Grafikwork; **296** Alina Demidenko, Marssanya; **297** Tsuguliev; **298** Marssanya, Vincent noel; **299** Africa Studio, stock photofan1, Kao; **305** Alex Staroseltsev; **308** EtiAmmos, LifetimeStock; **309** akiyoko; **312** Michele Bagdon; **313** Julia_Lelija; **314** D7INAMI7S; **316** Kletr; **318** artnLera, jantima14; **319** Nattika; **321** blue67design, JRP Studio; **324** Winiki; **325** mhatzapa, rsooll; **329** AlenKadr; **330** cubolabo, timquo; **332** James Steidl; **334** symbiot; **335** ducu59us; **338** Carolyn Franks; **340** SeDmi; **341** Vadym Zaitsev; **342** liskus; **345** Sarah2; **346** Andrey_Popov, Levent Konuk; **347** saruntorn chotchitima; **350** thodonal88; **351** Chayatorn Laorattanavech; **352** Chayatorn Laorattanavech, Erik D, fewerton; **355** primiaou, Valentyna7; **357** Tiger Images; **358** Lano4ka, Mr. SUTTIPON YAKHAM, Tiger Images; **360** Natasha Pankina, Sanit Fuangnakhon; **363** balabolka, cubolabo; **366** Keith Bell; **368** aarrows; **370** Dima Moroz' **372** Africa Studio; **373** JeniFoto; **374** Hong Vo, Photka, Tommy Atthi; **375** LoopAll; **376** Africa Studio; **378** Bscmediallc, timquo; **379** vincent noel; **380** Binh Thanh Bui; **382** Madlen; **384** Eric Isselee; **386** Sapnocte; **387** Africa Studio; **389** Cherdchai charasri; **394** Quang Ho; **400** Gencho Petkov; **402** Kelly vanDellen; **403** Design56; **406** Sofiaworld; **407** Perlav; **410** Ed Samuel; **413** Dmitry Polonskiy, Hdesislava, LukaKikina; **418** Tim UR; **424** Africa Studio, Quang Ho; **429** Andrey Lobachev, Birute Vijeikiene; **434** Dslaven; **435** Evikka, Mike Flippo; **436** COLOA Studio, Fablok, hitforsa; **437** Cunaplus unaplus; **438** Mayakova; **440** Maetisa; **441** Eivaisla; **442** Evikka; **443** Timquo; **444** Fotoearl, Petr Jilek; **447** KAMONRAT; **448** LanKS; **449** lenetstan; **450** Arthito; **451** Gino Santa Maria; **454** Lisovskaya Natalia; **455** Coprid; **456** Symbiot; **458** baibaz; **459** absolutimages, Natasha Pankina; **460** a_v_d; **462** tratong; **463** margouillat photo; **467** KucherAV; **468** Iriskana, Pixelbliss; **469** iamtui7; **470** 9comeback, Laurelie; **471** a_v_d, advent; **474–475** Trinset; **476** Africa Studio; **478** Mike Flippo; **479** Africa Studio; **480** The_Pixel; **481** MaraZe; **482** Erik D, Monticello; **484** Nataliia Pyzhova; **485** Happy monkey; **486** Diana Taliun, smilewithjul; **488** IB Photography; **489** FakeStocker; **490** Pixelbliss, Stockforlife; **491** Viktar Malyshchyts; **494** Christoforos Avramidis; **496** Motorolka, Rangizzz; **497** Motorolka; **498** Vinicius Tupinamba; **499** Madlen; **505** Ariya Phornpraphan; **508** Lano4ka, vesna cvorovic, zorina_larisa; **509** Pakula Piotr; **510** akepong srichaichana; **512** Roxana Bashyrova; **513** Bennian; **514** Istimages; **516** mkos83, Natasha Pankina; **518** Eric Isselee; **519** Danielle Balderas, Feng Yu; **520** M.Unal Ozmen; **527** Bjoern Wylezich; **529** Barry Blackburn, Tapui; **530** wk1003mike, Wonderful Future World; **531** Mlorenz, Viktor Kunz; **534** Alexandr Korolev, Natasha Pankina; **535** PrimaStockPhoto; **536** kudla, olnik_y; **538** mlorenz; **539** Voronina Svetlana; **540** Cipariss; **541** BERNATSKAYA OXANA, mhatzapa; **542** Bernatskaya Oxana, mhatzapa; **544** Vladimir Sazonov; **545** Eric Isselee, qingqing; **546** kanashi, mhatzapa; **547** Nikolai

©Curriculum Associates, LLC   Copying is not permitted.

Tsvetokov; **548** Mmaxer; **549** Africa Studio, artnLera; **551** Jiang Hongyan; **552** Hong Vo; **553** LuXpics; **554** Paket; **555** Hurst Photo; **556** Juburg; **557** Julie vanec; **558** Nik Merkulov; **560** Mrs_ya; **561** Nik Merkulov; **562** Valentyn Hontovyy; **564** HatzapaM; **566** artnLera, Elena Schweitzer; **568** Garsya, Natasha Pankina; **569** Hans Geel; **570** Kuznetsov Alexey; **572** Duplass, olnik_y; **575** Mircevski; **578** Galina Petrova; **580** Zoart Studio; **582** MaxFX; **586** T. Dallas; **590** Peter Hermes Furian; **596** Ed Lermey; **598** Butsaya; **601** Diana Taliun; **602** Gts; **604** Gts; **606** Kitch Bain; **608** Alexander Raths; **609** Natasha Pankina, Nearbirds; **615** Alexandru Nika; **619** Aila Images, M. Unal Ozmen; **622** jeep5d; **623** Eric Isselee, Nantawat Chotsuwan; **628** MirasWonderland; **634** Milya; **640** Gjermund; **641** Cartarium; **663** Africa Studio, Nubenamo; **664** Joe Belanger; **666** M. Unal Ozmen; **668** Keith Homan, Natasha Pankina; **671** Ifong; **674** Nuttapong; **675** Billion Photos; **676** Gresei; **678** Iriskana, Kitamin; **679** Cigdem; **680** Nata-Lia; **683** Africa Studio; **686** liskus; **688** Ivan Anta; **690** JeniFoto; **695** marssanya, Mellutto; **698** Bedrin; **700** Swill Klitch; **A5** Showcake; **A13** Trinacria Photo

©Curriculum Associates, LLC   Copying is not permitted.